FOR
YOUNG VOICES

SOMETHING TO
SING
ABOUT

G. SCHIRMER, INC.

Writers

Marsha Carlisle	Choir Director South Houston High School Pasadena ISD Houston, Texas
Lois B. Land	Professor Emeritus Southern Methodist University Dallas, Texas
Betty G. Roe	Choral Director McCullough High School Conroe ISD The Woodlands, Texas
Sally Schott	Choral Director South Houston High School Pasadena ISD Houston, Texas

Consultant

Rosemary Heffley	Southern Methodist University Dallas, Texas

Editor

Sally Schott

Special Contributors

Margaret Cavenagh
Dede Duson
Margaret Mathis

Publisher Consultant

Margaret Ross Griffel

Book design and illustration by N. Clayton

reg. 48603c
ed. 3465
ISBN: 0-911320-05-9

FOR
YOUNG VOICES

SOMETHING TO
SING
ABOUT

Time Line Chronology

The Historical View of the Arts

The Historical View of the Arts

EVENTS	MUSIC
B.C.	
Neanderthal Man	
THE OLD KINGDOM (Egypt, 2700-2200 B.C.)	
BEGINNING OF HELLENIC CIVILIZATION (c. 1100 B.C.)	
First Olympic Games (776 B.C.)	
Founding of Roman Republic (c. 500 B.C.)	Pythagoras explains mathematical relationship of musical tones.
Peloponnesian Wars (437-404 B.C.)	
Plato founds Academy (387 B.C.)	
Alexander the Great conquers known world (336-323 B.C.)	
Third Punic War; destruction of Carthage (150-146 B.C.)	
Athens sacked by Romans (86 B.C.)	
Julius Caesar becomes Dictator of Rome (49 B.C.)	
Defeat of Anthony and Cleopatra at Actium (31 B.C.)	
A.D.	
Edict of Milan legalizes Christianity (313 A.D.)	
Byzantium capital of East Roman Empire (324-330 A.D.)	
Fall of West Roman Empire (476 A.D.)	Pope Grepory the Great establishes Gregorian chant for Roman Catholic liturgy (about 600).
Moorish Conquest of Spain (711-715)	Music culitvated in monasteries, abbeys.
Charlemagne crowned Holy Roman Emperor (800)	
FEUDALISM (900-1200)	Earliest sacred polyphony begins (2- and 3-part organum).
1000	Guido of Arezzo establishes basis of modern staff notation.
Mayan culture centers in northern Yucatán (1000)	
Leif Eriksen reaches North America (c. 1000)	
William of Normandy conquers England (1066)	
Pope Gregory VII (1073-1085)	
1100	Troubadour and Trouvère songs—beginnings of secular art song.
PERIOD OF CRUSADES (11th-14th century)	Leonin and Perotin develop early sacred polyphony at Notre Dame in Paris.
1200	
Francis of Assisi founds Franciscan Order (1210)	Minnesingers active in Germany.
AGE OF CHIVALRY (12th and 13th c.)	
Magna Carta (1215)	"Sumer is Icumen in"—oldest surviving piece of secular polyphony.
Louis IX, golden age of medieval France (1226-1270)	
Marco Polo brings Europe knowledge of Asia (1275-1292)	
BEGINNING OF RENAISSANCE	

2

From EXPLORING MUSIC, "The Senior Book," by Beth Landis
Copyright © 1969 by Holt, Rinehart and Winston, Publishers
Used by permission.

VISUAL ARTS	LITERATURE

Cave Paintings

The Pyramids (Egypt)

Old Testament

GREEK
Golden Age (480-404 B.C.)
Parthenon   Spear Bearer by Polyclitus
Elgin Marbles   Discus Thrower by Myron

Hellenistic (2nd-1st Century B.C.)
Venus de Milo   Winged Victory of Samothrace
Laocoön

CLASSICAL BEGINNINGS
  (500 B.C.-500 A.D.)
    GREECE

DRAMATISTS	PHILOSOPHERS	
Aeschylus	Socrates	
Sophocles	Plato	
Euripides	Aristotle	
Aristophanes		

POETS	FABULIST	HISTORIANS
Homer	Aesop	Herodotus
Heslod		Xenophon
Sappho		Plutarch

ROME
Golden Age

POETS
Vergil
Horace
Ovid

EARLY CHRISTIAN (A.D.-1000)   **ROMAN**
Catacombs   Colosseum
Old St. Peter's   Arch of
                                      Constantine

Byzantine Style
St. Sophia
Churches at Ravenna (Italy)

Decline

POETS	PHILOSOPHER	ECCLESIASTICAL
Juvenal	Plotinus	WRITERS
Boethius		Ambrose
		Jerome
		Augustine

ISLAMIC STYLE
Mosque at Córdoba (Spain) 8thC
Alhambra Palace (Granada) 14thC
ROMANESQUE (mid 11th-12th Centuries)
Cluny Monastery Complex
Pisa Cathedral, Baptistery and Tower

CHRISTIAN, CLASSICAL, AND
  MYTHIC TRADITIONS (700-1400)
Italy

POETS	ECCLESIASTICAL
Petrarch	WRITER
Dante	Thomas Aquinas
Boccaccio	

France
POETS
Guillaume de Lorris and
Jean de Meun ''Romance of
  the Rose''

EVENTS	MUSIC
1300	Guillaume de Machaut (France)—composed ''Notre Dame'' Mass—first polyphonic Mass written by one individual.
Expansion of Inca Empire to Chile (1300) Aztecs control Central and South Mexico (1325-1500) Black Death sweeps Europe (1348) Great Schism (1378-1417)	Italy and France develop secular vocal forms (madrigal, ballata).
	Instruments (viols, ancient brass, wind, and organ) used to double or elaborate on vocal works, or to accompany dances.
1400	Music flourishes at Burgundian court; Masses, motets, secular chansons Dufay, Binchois prominent.
Joan of Arc burned at the stake (1431) End of the Hundred Years' War (1337-1453)	
1450	
Constantinople falls to Turks (1453) War of the Roses (1455) Beginning of the House of Tudor (1485-1603) Columbus discovers the New World (1492) Vasco da Gama rounds Cape of Good Hope (1498)	Netherlands School (1450-1550)—brings Renaissance polyphony to height. Ockeghem Josquin des Près Heinrich Isaac Obrecht Orlando di Lasso
1500	Protestant church music (chorale settings) begins in Germany. Martin Luther Johann Walther
AGE OF EXPLORATION Beginning of Protestant Reformation (1517) Magellan's ships go around the world (1519-1522) Henry VIII reigns in England (1509-1547)	Roman School Cristóbal Morales (Spain) Victoria (Spain) Palestrina—perfected disciplined, serene liturgical style.
Charles I of Spain made Holy Roman Emperor (1519)	Renaissance madrigal reaches height of development.
Fall of Inca Empire (1533)	Golden Age of English Music (1525-1625) Thomas Tallis Orlando Gibbons Thomas Tomkins William Byrd John Wilbye
Beginning of Counter Reformation (1534) Church of England separates from Rome (1534)	Independent instrumental styles emerge in fantasia, ricercare, canzona, dance forms; harpsichord, lute music popular.
1550	Tonal harmony begins to replace modes.
Council of Trent (1545-1563) Elizabeth reigns in England (1558-1603)	Shift of emphasis begins from polyphony to chordal styles. Giovanni Gabrieli (Venice)—developed multichoral style.
English sink Spanish Armada (1588)	Monteverdi (Italy)—first notable composer of opera, renowned madrigalist.
1600	*Euridice*, first opera, by Peri and Caccini, performed in Florence, 1600. Early instrumental suites develop in Germany.
Settlement of Jamestown (1607) Mayflower lands at Plymouth Rock (1620) Philip IV reigns in Spain (1621-1665) Thirty Years' War (1616-1648) Administration of Cardinal Richelieu (1624-1642) Treaty of Westphalia (1648)	Oratorio, cantata develop.

4

VISUAL ARTS

GOTHIC (13th-14th centuries and later)
Notre Dame Cathedral
Chartres Cathedral
Salisbury Cathedral

GOTHIC PRE-RENAISSANCE
(mid 13th-14th centuries) Italy
Duccio—A leader of the Siennese School
Giotto—Founder of the Renaissance style

RENAISSANCE
(15th-16th C.)
Italy
PAINTERS
Fra Angelico
Uccello
Masaccio
Piero della Francesca
Botticelli

SCULPTORS
Ghilberti
Donatello

ARCHITECTS
Brunelleschi

NORTHERN RENAISSANCE
PAINTERS
Hubert and Jan van Eyck
  (Flanders)
van der Goes (Flanders)

Cranach, the Elder
  (Germany)
Dürer (Germany)
Grünewald (Germany)
Holbein, the Younger
  (Germany)
Pieter Brueghel,
  the Elder (Flanders)

PAINTERS
Leonardo da Vinci
Raphael
Andrea del Sarto

SCULPTORS
Michelangelo (painter,
  sculptor, architect)
Cellini

ARCHITECTS
Bramante
Palladio

Taj Mahal (India)
1630-1648

PRE-COLUMBIAN (Central
  and South American
  Indian Civilizations)

Maya (c. 100 BC-1697 AD)
Inca (c. 1200-1533)
Aztec (late 12thC-1525)
Toltec (c. 900-13thC)

LITERATURE

England
Beowolf
Arthurian Legends
Geoffrey Chaucer
Piers Plowman

THE RISE OF EUROPEAN LITERATURES
  (1400-1700)

Italy
Niccolo Machiavelli
Lorenzo de' Medici

Spain
NOVELIST
Miguel de Cervantes

DRAMATIST
Lope de Vega

France
POET
François Villon

DRAMATISTS
Corneille
Racine
Molière

PHILOSOPHER
René Descartes

England
POETS
Sir Thomas Malory
Sir Phillip Sidney
Edmund Spenser
John Donne
John Milton
John Dryden

DRAMATISTS
Marlowe
Shakespeare
Ben Jonson

ALLEGORY AND FICTION
John Bunyan
Daniel Defoe

ESSAYISTS
Addison and Steele

MORAL PHILOSOPHERS
Thomas Hobbes
Francis Bacon
Sir Thomas Browne

PHILOSOPHER
John Locke

PHYSICIST
Sir Isaac Newton

EVENTS	MUSIC

EVENTS

1650

6

Reign of Louis XIV (1648-1715)
Oliver Cromwell rules England
  (1653-1658)
Restoration of the British monarchy (1660)
Black Death sweeps London (1664-1665)
Newton discovers Law of Gravity (1666)

Revocation of the Edict of Nantes (1685)
Glorious Revolution; William and Mary
  (1688)

1700

AGE OF REASON (18th C.)
War of the Spanish Succession
  (1701-1714)
Death of Louis XIV (1715)
Louis XV, King of France (1715-1774)
Maria Theresa, Empress of Austria
  (1740-1780)

Frederick the Great, King of Prussia
  (1740-1786)

1750

American Declaration of Independence
  (1776)

English defeat French claims in India
  (1754-1761)

Seven Years' War (1756-1763)
Catherine the Great, Empress of Russia
  (1762-1796)

French Revolution (1789)
Napoleon leads campaign in Egypt (1798)

MUSIC

New instrumental forms emerge: orchestral suite, trio sonata, concerto, keyboard sonata, fugue.

Frescobaldi (Italy)

Opera and ballet flourish in France.
  Lully (court of Louis XIV)   Rameau

Protestant church music flourishes in Germany: chorales, cantatas, chorale-preludes, Passions.
  Heinrich Schütz   Buxtehude   J. S. Bach

Henry Purcell (England)

Increasing organization of harmonic system gives music new formal structure.

Italian craftsmen perfect modern string instruments.

Italian composers develop concerto grosso.
  Corelli   Vivaldi

François Couperin (le Grand)—leading composer of French keyboard school; develops ornamental style.

Italian Baroque opera gains in sumptuousness, virtuosity.
  Alessandro Scarlatti, Pergolesi *(opera buffa)*

Domenico Scarlatti (Italy)—innovator in keyboard music.

Pianoforte develops.

George Frideric Handel (Germany, England)— operas, oratorios, instrumental music.

Johann Sebastian Bach (Germany)—brought Baroque styles to their culmination.

Gluck (Germany)—developed new dramatic style in opera.

C. P. E. Bach—son of J. S. Bach, innovating composer and theorist.

Classical instrumental (Viennese) style develops.
  Joseph Haydn (Austria), Luigi Boccherini (Italy), Wolfgang Amadeus Mozart (Austria)
Classical Operatic Composers
  Cimarosa (Italy), Cherubini (Italy)
  Mozart—brought *opera buffa* to its culmination.

VISUAL ARTS

BAROQUE (17th C.)
PAINTERS
El Greco (Spain)
Caravaggio (Italy)
Rubens (Flanders)
George de la Tour
  (France)
Poussin (France)
Velázquez (Spain)
Van Dyck (Flanders)
Rembrandt (Holland)
Vermeer (Holland)
Claude Lorrain
  (France)

ARCHITECTS
Bernini (Italy) sculptor
  and architect
Christopher Wren
  (England)

INFLUENCE OF CHINESE ART ON WEST (17th-18th centuries)
DYNASTIES
T'ang (618-906)
  noted for: Sculpture
Sung (960-1279)
  noted for: Landscape
  painting
  Wen T'ung
  Ma Fen
  Ma Yuan
Ming (1365-1644)
  noted for: pottery

ROCOCO (18th C.)
PAINTERS
Watteau (France)
Tiepolo (Italy)
Hogarth (England)—
  graphic artist
Boucher (France)
Fragonard (France)

ENGLISH PORTRAIT PAINTERS
Reynolds
Romney
Gainsborough

Goya (1746-1828, Spain)—Rococo art, social satire, realism, fantasy and nightmare visions are present in his work.
Daumier (1808-1879, France)—social satire
Millet (1814-1875, France)—social realism
Courbet (1819-1877, France)—realsim

NEO-CLASSICAL (1750-1850)
PAINTERS
David (France)
Ingres (France)
SCULPTORS
Antonio Canova (Italy)

ROMANTIC (1820-1860)
PAINTERS
Delacroix (France)

LITERATURE

THE NEO-CLASSIC AGE
THE AGE OF REASON (1700-1800)

France	Germany	
PHILOSOPHER	POETS	PHILOSOPHER
Voltare	Goethe	Emmanuel Kant
Rousseau	Schiller	

England
SATIRISTS AND NOVELISTS
Jonathan Swift
Horace Walpole
Henry Fielding
Jane Austen

BIOGRAPHER
James Boswell

DRAMATISTS
Sheridan
Goldsmith

POETS
Alexander Pope
William Blake

MORAL PHILOSOPHER, ESSAYIST
AND POET—Samuel Johnson

THE ROMANTIC AND VICTORIAN AGES (1800-1900)
ROMANTIC

Germany	POETS	Denmark
PHILOSOPHER	Hoffmann	PHILOSOPHER
Hegel	Hölderlin	Kierkegaard

EVENTS	MUSIC

EVENTS

1800

Louisiana Purchase (1803)
Napoleon crowned emperor (1804)

War of 1812
The Congress of Vienna (1814)

WESTWARD EXPANSION IN
    AMERICA
Napoleon defeated in Battle of Waterloo
    (1815)
The Hapsburg Monarchy (1815-1848)
The Monroe Doctrine (1823)

PERIOD OF REVOLUTIONS
The July Revolution in Paris (1830)
The Belgian Revolution (1830)
Era of Reform in England (1823-1846)
Victoria reigns in England (1837-1901)
Treaty of Nanking (1842)
Mexican-American War (1846-1848)
California Gold Rush (1848)
The Italian War of Independence
    (1848-1849)

1850

The Crimean War (1853-1856)
Admiral Perry opens Japan (1854)
Bismarck, Chancellor of Prussia
    (1862-1890)
The Civil War (1860-1865)
Karl Marx; Internat'l Workingmen's Assoc.
    (1864)
Opening of Suez Canal (1869)
Franco-Prussian War (1870)
Unification of Italy (1849-1870)
Disraeli and Gladstone, prime ministers
    (1863-1894)
Alexander Graham Bell invents telephone
    (1876)
The Third Republic, France (1870-1940)
Pasteur develops milk "pasteurization"
    (1885)
Freud studies the subconscious (1895)
The Spanish-American War (1898)
The Boer War, South Africa (1899)

1900

Boxer Rebellion in China (1900)
First successful airplane flight (1903)
Russian-Japanese War (1904-1905)

MUSIC

Sonata-allegro form perfected and dominates new instrumental works (symphonies, piano sonatas, string quartets).

Ludwig van Beethoven (Germany)—exemplified best of both Classical and Romantic styles.

Virtuosity becomes important in instrumental music: virtuoso performer-composers idolized (Paganini, Liszt, Chopin).

Small piano works and *lieder* become expressive forms.

Early German Romantics	Romantic Opera	
Schubert	von Weber	Verdi
Mendelssohn	Meyerbeer	Wagner
Schumann	Rossini	Gounod
	Donizetti	Bizet
	Bellini	Puccini
	Offenbach	

French Romantics
    Hector Berlioz—innovator
    in new uses of orchestral
    tone color.
    César Franck
    Saint-Saëns

Solo concerto becomes one of the most popular forms of Romantic expression.

Ballet develops further, gains in brilliance, virtuosity.
Tchaikovsky (Russia)—symphonies, ballets.

Musical designs expand and are used with greater freedom; massive and exotic tone colors exploited.

Program music becomes popular.

Late German Romantics	Nationalism
	Borodin (Russia)
Brahms	Mussorgsky (Russia)
Bruckner (Austria)	Dvořák (Czechoslovakia)
Hugo Wolf (Austria)	Grieg (Norway)
Mahler (Austria)	Rimsky-Korsakov (Russia)
Richard Strauss	Sibelius (Finland)

Debussy (France)—foremost exponent of musical impressionism.
Ravel (France)—brilliant orchestrator.

VISUAL ARTS

ARCHITECTS
Thomas Jefferson
(United States)
Latrobe (U.S.)

Géricault (France)
Ingres (France)
also influenced:
England
Turner and Constable
France
Barbizon School—
Corot and Millet
United States
Hudson River School

JAPANESE ART INFLUENCES
IMPRESSIONISTS

PAINTERS
Fuglwara no Yorimichi (11thC)
Sesson Shokel (16thC)
Hasegawa Tôhaku (17thC)
Korin (17thC)
GRAPHIC ARTISTS (18thC)
Harunobu
Sharaku
Utamaro
Hiroshige
Hokusai

IMPRESSIONISM (1860-1910)

PAINTERS
Manet (France)
Monet (France)
Degas (France)
Renoir (France)
Toulouse-Lautrec
(France)
Sisley (France)
Mary Cassatt (U.S.)
also influenced:
Whistler (U.S.)
Rodin (France) sculptor

POST IMPRESSIONISM
PAINTERS
Seurat (France)
Cézanne (France)
Van Gogh (Holland, France)
Gauguin (France)

PRIMITIVES

PAINTERS
Hicks (U.S.)
Henri Rousseau (France)

AFRICAN and OCEANIC SCULPTURE influences Picasso and the Cubist movement.

Picasso (Spain, France) painter, sculptor

LITERATURE

France

NOVELISTS		POETS
Stendhal	Hugo	Baudelaire
Balzac	Flaubert	Musset, Gautier
	Dumas	

America
POETS
H. W. Longfellow
Edgar Allan Poe

PHILOSOPHERS
Ralph Waldo Emerson
Henry David Thoreau

NOVELIST   Hawthorne

England

POETS	NOVELISTS
Wordsworth	Sir Walter Scott
Coleridge	Emily Brontë
Keats	Charlotte Brontë
Shelley	W. M. Thackeray
Byron	Charles Dickens

ESSAYIST AND HISTORIAN   Thomas Carlyle

VICTORIAN AND LATE 19TH CENTURY

Germany	Norway	Scotland
PHILOSOPHERS	DRAMATIST	NOVELIST
Friedrich Nietzsche	Ibsen	Robert Louis
Karl Marx	Sweden	Stevenson
Friedrich Engels	DRAMATIST	
	Strindberg	

France

POETS	NOVELISTS
Mallarmé, Verlaine	Zola, Anatole France
Rimbaud	Proust, George Sand

STORY WRITER   de Maupassant

Russia
NOVELISTS
Dostoevski, Tolstoy

DRAMATIST
Chekov

America

POETS	NOVELISTS
Emily Dickinson	Mark Twain
Walt Whitman	Herman Melville
James Russell Lowell	Henry James
PHILOSOPHER	STORY WRITER
William James	O. Henry

England

POETS	NOVELISTS
Alfred Lord Tennyson	Thomas Hardy
Robert Browning	George Eliot
D. G. Rossetti	Rudyard Kipling
Swinburne	STORY WRITERS
G. M. Hopkins	Saki (H. H. Munro)
DRAMATIST Oscar Wilde	Lewis Carroll

THE TWENTIETH CENTURY

Russia   POLITICAL PHILOSOPHER   Lenin

POETS	NOVELISTS
Boris Pasternak	Mikail Sholokhov
Evgeny Evtushenko	Alexander Solzhenitzyn

EVENTS	MUSIC

EVENTS

First sound moving picture (1904)
Einstein offers Theory of Relativity (1905)
Peary reaches North Pole (1909)

Discovery of the South Pole (1910-1912)
Outbreak of the Chinese Revolution (1911)
Opening of the Panama Canal (1914)

Bolshevik Revolution (1917)

World War I (1914-1918)
Treaty of Versailles (1919)
First assembly of League of Nations (1920)
Women's Suffrage (19th Amendment) (1920)
Lindbergh's flight from New York to Paris (1927)
First transmission of television signals (1927)
Collapse of the stockmarket (1929)
Nazi Revolution (1933)
New Deal legislation (1933-1936)
Spanish Civil War (1936)
Franco controls Spain (1939-1975)
World War II (1939-1945)
Possibility of splitting atom shown (1940)
Pearl Harbor (1941)
Invasion of Normandy (1944)
Atomic bomb dropped on Hiroshima (1945)
First assembly of United Nations (1946)
War between Israel and Arab League (1948)
Establishment of NATO (1949)
People's Republic of China proclaimed (1949)

1950

Korean Conflict (1950-1953)
Emergence of African nations (1950-1965)
Vietnam War (1950-1975)
Death of Stalin (1953)
Launching of first earth satellite (1957)
de Gaulle, Pres. of French Republic (1959-1969)
First successful weather satellite (1960)
Man's first successful orbital space flight (1961)
Telstar (1962)
Assassination of John F. Kennedy (1963)
Man's first ''walk'' outside spaceship (1965)
Man first orbits the moon (1968)

MUSIC

Stravinsky's *Rite of Spring* premiered in Paris (1913).
Jazz begins to flourish.
Group of French composers reacts against Romanticism.
  Satie Milhaud Honegger Poulenc
Musical comedies gain in popularity.
Schoenberg's first twelve-tone works appear (1924).
Alban Berg, Anton von Webern further develop twelve-tone technique.
New concepts of form, harmony, melody, and rhythm gain precedence over traditional sounds.

Stravinsky (Russia, U.S.)—spans primitive, neo-Classic, and twelve-tone techniques.

Bartók (Hungary, U.S.)—opens new paths by combining East European folk idioms with Western contemporary techniques.

Hindemith (Germany, U.S.)—neo-Classicist; developed new system of harmonic theory.
Other twentieth-century European composers
  Rachmaninoff (Russia, U.S.)
  Holst (England)
  Respighi (Italy)
  Bloch (Switzerland, U.S.)
  Ralph Vaughan Williams (England)
  Kodály (Hungary, U.S.)
  Prokofiev (Russia)
  Off (Germany)
  Walton (English)
  Shostakovitch (Russia)
  Benjamin Britten (England)
  Hans-Werner Henze (Germany)
Twentieth-century American composers

Villa-Lobos (Brazil)	Aaron Copland
Virgil Thomson	Elliott Carter
Roger Sessions	Samuel Barber
Walter Piston	Norman Dello Jolo
George Gershwin	Leonard Bernstein
Carlos Chávez (Mexico)	Lukas Foss

Some early twentieth-century experimentalists—
  Charles Ives (U.S.)
  Henry Cowell (U.S.)
  Edgard Varèse (France, U.S.)
  Harry Partch (U.S.)
—pave way for later innovators
  John Cage (U.S.)
  Milton Babbitt (U.S.)
  Pierre Boulez (France)
  Karlheinz Stockhausen (Germany)

VISUAL ARTS

CUBISM

Braque (France)
Léger (France)
Gris (Spain)
  also influenced:
Mondrian
  (Holland, U.S.)
Modigliani (Italy)
  painter, sculptor
Max Weber (U.S.)

EXPRESSIONIST SCHOOLS

Munch (Norway)
Kandinsky (Russia,
  Germany, U.S.)
Klee (Switzerland)
Rouault (France)
Beckmann (Germany)
Willem de Kooning
  (Holland, U.S.)
Jackson Pollock (U.S.)
  also influenced:
Matisse (France)

SURREALISM—The expression of imagination as revealed in dreams, free of conscious control or convention.

Max Ernst (Germany)
Dali (Spain)
Miró (Spain)

also influenced:
Chagall (Russia, France, U.S.)

FUTURISM—The expression of dynamic energy and movement associated with mechanical processes.

Joseph Stella (U.S.)
Marcel Duchamp (France, U.S.)

SOCIAL REALISM

Orozco (Mexico)
Ben Shahn (U.S.)
Andrew Wyeth (U.S.)

Realistic style:
Grant Wood (U.S.)

POP ART

Marcel Duchamp
  (France, U.S.)
George Segal (U.S.)
Roy Lichtenstein (U.S.)
Andy Warhol (U.S.)

OP ART

Albers (Germany, U.S.)
Vasarely (France)
Bridget Riley (England)
Larry Poons (U.S.)

SCULPTORS

Brancusi (France)
Arp (France)
Lipschitz (U.S.)
Calder (U.S.)
Moore (England)
Epstein (U.S., England)
Giacometti
  (Switzerland)
David Smith (U.S.)

ARCHITECTS

Antonio Gaudí (Spain)
Louis Sullivan (U.S.)
Frank Lloyd Wright (U.S.)
Gropius (Germany)
Mies van der Rohe
  (Germany, U.S.)
Le Corbusier
  (Switzerland, France)
Nervi (Italy)
Buckminster Fuller (U.S.)
Johnson (U.S.)
Eero Saarinen
  (Finland, U.S.)
Marcel Breuer (Germany, U.S.)

LITERATURE

Germany

NOVELISTS	POET
Franz Kafka	Rainer Maria Rilke
Thomas Mann	DRAMATIST
Hermann Hesse	Bertolt Brecht

France

NOVELISTS	DRAMATISTS	PHILOSOPHER
André Maurois	Jean Giraudoux	Jean-Paul Sartre
Albert Camus	Jean Cocteau	
André Gide	Paul Claudel	
André Malraux	Jean Genêt	

Ireland

POET	NOVELIST	DRAMATISTS
William Butler Yeats	James Joyce	G. B. Shaw
		Sean O'Casey

England

NOVELISTS	POETS	DRAMATISTS
Ford Madox Ford	T. S. Eliot	John Osborne
Joseph Conrad	W. H. Auden	Harold Pinter
D. H. Lawrence	Edith Sitwell	
W. Somerset Maugham	Stephen Spender	HISTORIANS
Aldous Huxley	Robert Graves	Sir Winston Churchill
John Galsworthy		Arnold
George Orwell	PHILOSOPHER	Toynbee
E. M. Forster	Bertrand Russell	
C. P. Snow		

America

NOVELISTS	PHILOSOPHER	POETS
Sinclair Lewis	John Dewey	E. A. Robinson
John Dos Passos		Robert Frost
Thomas Wolfe	STORY WRITERS	Carl Sandburg
F. Scott Fitzgerald	Ambrose Bierce	Hart Crane
Ernest Hemingway	John Cheever	Gertrude Stein
William Faulkner	DRAMATISTS	Ezra Pound
John O'Hara	Tennessee Williams	e. e. cummings
John Barth		Conrad Aiken
Vladimir Nabokov	Eugene O'Neill	Robert Lowell
HUMORISTS		Richard Eberhart
Ring Lardner	JOURNALISTS	
Groucho Marx	E. B. White	
Ogden Nash	Edward R. Murrow	
W. C. Fields	William L. Shirer	
James Thurber		

Austria	Wales	Greece
PSYCHOLOGIST	POET	NOVELIST
Sigmund Freud	Dylan Thomas	N. Kazantzakis

Switzerland	Italy	India
PSYCHOLOGIST	DRAMATISTS	POET
Carl Jung	Luigi Pirandello	Rabindranath Tagore
	Federico Fellini	

The Development of Choral Music

Choral music can be described as music which is written for a chorus or choir, or music which is intended to be sung by more than one singer to each individual part. While the art of choral music had its early beginnings in Greek music, Jewish music, and early Christian worship, choral singing as we know it today has only existed for the last 200 years.

Throughout the long history of the development of choral music, the number of parts for which it was written has grown from one for unison singing to an unlimited number of voice parts. Choral music is written for treble voices only, male voices only, or treble and male voices in various combinations. In addition, some choral music is designed to be performed by small choirs with one or two singers on each voice part, or by very large choirs of two hundred singers or more. Choral music can be written for one, two, or several choirs, again in various combinations of voice parts. Some choral music is written to be sung a cappella (without instrumental accompaniment), and some is written to be performed with instrumental accompaniment.

Choral music can be divided into two main categories according to the content of the text: *sacred music* (music that is written to be sung in a worship service or that has religious meaning) and *secular music* (music whose text is "worldly" or does not relate religious ideas).

Choral Music in Antiquity and the Middle Ages

Historians have very little firsthand knowledge of early music of the ancient world, first because it was not written down and second, because most of it was freely improvised. Art of the period and treatises on music give evidence of the importance of music in the life of early Greece. Music played a vital role in Grecian drama, brought grandeur to governmental ceremonies, heightened the passion of Greek poetry, called men to battle, and, most important, was crucial to the religious ritual. Early Greek music consisted of a single line of melody sung in octaves and sometimes accompanied by stringed instruments.

MUSIC OF THE EARLY CHURCH

Offering praise to God through singing was a vital part of the Hebrew culture. The Old Testament gives numerous accounts of organized singing in ancient Israel. The Book of Chronicles accounts for a systematic musical culture, centered in the Temple and organized by the Levites who were appointed to supply 4,000 musicians for the religious services. A choir school was organized and maintained to train the *cantors* (soloists) and the *choristers* (singers in the choir) for the Temple. Early choral performances in the Temple consisted of *antiphonal* (alternating choirs) and *responsorial* singing (alternation of choir and soloist). The congregations of the Temple rarely participated in the service but would occasionally respond with short verbal statements such as "amen" or "hallelujah." The music of the early church was prepared and performed by professional singers who were paid and who were furnished homes.

The early Christian Church followed the practices of the Jewish Temple in that the singing was responsorial or antiphonal. When Christianity was recognized as an official religion in 313, St. Sylvester, who was Pope from 314 to 336, founded the first singing school or *schola cantorum*. The school was dedicated to the instruction and training of singers for the papal choir. Eventually the monasteries became dedicated to the training of basic musical skills and served as the centers of early choral music education.

GREGORIAN CHANT

The first musical center for Christian music was in Milan where Bishop Ambrose was the first to write down a uniform collection of songs and texts (*Ambrosian chants*) for Church use. Two centuries later, Pope Gregory I (reigned 590-604) undertook a similar task of greater importance and proportion. He reformed the liturgy of the Church and established a uniform repertoire of 3,000 chants for specific use by the Roman Catholic Church. The chants (which came to be known as *Gregorian chants*) follow the calendar of the Roman Catholic Church and are especially important because they are the musical inspiration for the later development of important musical forms, particularly the Mass and motet.

MELODY

Until the ninth century, vocal music was limited to single line melodies which were usually sung without instrumental accompaniment. At the turn of the century the single line melodies were enriched by parallel melodic lines usually at the interval of a fourth or fifth below the primary melody. At first, the second part was merely a shadow of the primary melody but gradually more freedom was given to the second part. Eventually the parts were expanded to three parts, each of which gained rhythmic and harmonic independence.

FUNCTION OF MUSIC

In the churches and monasteries of the Middle Ages, the choirs were made up of men only or of men and boys; women were able to sing sacred music only in a convent. The early cathedral choirs usually consisted of from four to six boys and from ten to thirteen men. In the late Middle Ages the use of instruments with voices returned to the worship service (banned earlier by order of the Pope). Many churches had organs, and string and wind instruments were used regularly in processions outside the church and occasionally inside the church. The organ and other instruments played in alternation with the a cappella voices. It was not until the late fourteenth century that voices were used in combination with instruments.

MUSICAL NOTATION

The period from 1100 to about 1400 has been categorized as Gothic, mainly because of the influence of the architecture of the period. Cathedrals built during this time are identified by their pointed arches, ribbed vaulting, and flying buttresses. The most important musical development of the Gothic period was the development of a system of musical notation. The musical staff on which the notes were written was developed in the twelfth century but there remained a need to identify the duration and stress of the notes on the staff. The organized system of musical notation made it possible for composers to record pitch, duration, and stress; dynamics, tempo markings, key signatures, and time signatures were not yet in existence. Although the music of the fourteenth century would be impossible to read today, it can be translated by scholars into modern musical notation.

The Renaissance (1400-1600)

The fifteenth century generally represents the transition from the Middle Ages to the Renaissance. Musical development in the Renaissance grew from a system of patronage. Composers of the period were hired by large churches or by royal courts to provide the music for their needs. The Burgundian courts of Philip the Good (1419-1467) and Charles the Bold (1467-1477) gave great support to the art of music. Their patronage of music moved the center of musical development from France and Italy to the Netherlands where a group of composers known as the *Burgundian School* dominated the development of musical style during the first part of the fifteenth century (Guillaume Dufay-ca. 1400-1474 and Gilles Binchois-ca. 1400-1460).

THE FLEMISH SCHOOL

The Burgundian Court (eastern France, Belgium, and the Netherlands) at Dijon was the leading cultural center for Western Europe. Musical style in the second half of the century was pioneered by another group of composers who came to be known as the *Flemish School*. Unlike the composers of the Burgundian School who were connected with the Burgundian Court, the composers of the Flemish School include a long list of those who came from southern Netherlands (present-day Belgium) and moved to other countries. Their influence was extraordinary because they stimulated a rise in national talent in countries such as France, Germany, Austria, Italy, England, Spain, Poland, and Hungary where they held important musical positions in large churches or in royal courts.

The greatest of the Flemish composers, Orlando di Lasso (1532-1594), was called the "Belgian Orpheus" and "The Prince of Music." He held important musical positions in several countries and was therefore known by several names: Roland de Lassus (Belgian), Orlando di Lasso (Italian), Orlandus Lassus (Latin), and Rolande de Lattre (French).

HUMANISM

The term "Renaissance," like "Gothic" for the late Middle Ages and "Baroque" for the 150 years following the Renaissance, was borrowed from art history. Its literal meaning, "rebirth," appropriately categorizes the artists, sculptors, and architects who looked to the past achievements of the ancient world of Greece and Rome to create masterpieces in their own time. The term is somewhat misleading in that it implies a sudden rebirth and awakening of the arts and of learning in a world covered by the ignorance and cultural void of the Middle Ages. History moves slowly and, upon reflection, it can be loosely organized into certain groupings of time according to pattern changes in daily life, culture, history, and science.

The Renaissance marks a significant change from a sacred-oriented society to a society that was secularly oriented, a society in which man, not God, was the central figure. The rebirth was an awakening of the human spirit. "Humanism," as it was called, stressed the virtues of the living man. The Renaissance writers and poets spread the ideal that man had rights, inner strengths, and worthy personal feelings. Humanist writers began to use secular subject matter so that their works might be acceptable not only to God through their religious writings, but also to living men through their secular writings.

The high Renaissance produced such great artists as da Vinci, Michelangelo, Titian, Dürer, and Holbein. Literature matched artistic greatness with Machiavelli in Italy, Rabelais, Montaigne, and Ronsard in France, Cervantes in Spain, and Shakespeare, Spencer, Bacon, and Ben Johnson in England. The field of science felt the awakening spirit in Copernicus and Galileo. Explorers such as Columbus were eager to discover the world around them. Religion also underwent a major change in the form of the Protestant Reformation, led by Martin Luther.

MUSIC PRINTING

The rise of music printing was especially important to the development of music. The practice of printing books from movable type, as perfected by Johann Gutenberg in 1450, was applied to music printing. The first collection of music printed from movable type was published in 1501 by Ottaviano de'Petrucci in Venice.

THE VENETIAN SCHOOL

The great cathedral of St. Mark's in Venice became important as the center for an important group of composers of the Renaissance known as the Venetian School. Their unique style of composition was directly related to the architecture of the cathedral. Built in the eleventh century, the plan of the church is a Greek cross of equal arms, covered by a large central dome and by a dome over each of the arms of the cross. The two domes of the church (facing each other) served as choir lofts, each with its own organ. The architectural plan, with its spacious interior, rounded domes, and gold mosaics, inspired the composers who served as *Maestro di Cappella* (Choirmaster). The cathedral was the chapel of the Doge, the ruler of the small independent city state of Venice.

The music of the composers of the Venetian School has three important characteristics which are directly influenced by either the architecture of the cathedral or by the splendor of the city of Venice:

1. Music that is written for two or more choirs (*polychoral*) who sing alternately or together in a blend of chordal and imitative musical textures.

2. Rich textures of choral sound (men's voices and women's voices used in alternation or mixed voices in alternating choirs) and contrasting textures of voices and instruments.

3. Boldness of harmonies.

The greatest of the Venetian composers was Giovanni Gabrieli (1557-1612), nephew of Andrea Gabrieli (ca. 1510-1586). Giovanni Gabrieli's music expanded the Venetian style to include up to five choirs (one for each of the domes in St. Mark's), each with different combinations of high and low voices and each combined with instruments of different timbres. Gabrieli's music marks the first use of the words *piano* and *forte* which he used to indicate solo (piano) or tutti (forte) statements.

The Venetian School was admired as the most progressive in all of Italy, and it was an important influence on other composers of the Renaissance. Pupils of the Gabrielis came to Venice to study and carried the influence of their teachers to their native countries: Germany was represented by Heinrich Schütz (1585-1672), Hieronymus Praetorius (1560-1629), and Hans Leo Hassler (1524-1612); Czechoslovakia by Jacob Handl or Jacobus Gallus (1550-1591), and Italy by Claudio Monteverdi (1567-1643).

THE PROTESTANT REFORMATION

Perhaps the most dramatic event in the history of Christian religion was the Protestant Reformation of the sixteenth century. The Reformation was a revolt against many of the long-standing practices of the Roman Catholic Church. Because it was a religious revolt, it affected the music of the church and had a strong influence on the development of musical style. Led by Martin Luther (1483-1546), the conflict was centered in Germany but it spread quickly to other countries, especially France and England. Luther had strong feelings about the importance of music in the church. His main concern was that the music did not directly involve the congregation and that the continued use of Latin as the church language could not speak directly to the people. His reforms included many important principles: first, he substituted the traditional Latin words of the church ritual with German words; second, he encouraged congregational participation in the worship service through responsive readings and prayers; and third, he introduced hymn singing in the church. Until this time, all of the music in the church had been prepared by professional musicians. The *chorale* or *Kirchenlied* (church song), as it was called, was a hymn with German words set to a melody in verse fashion and sung by the entire congregation. The chorale became the backbone of the Lutheran worship service and inspired great composers such as Heinrich Schütz and Johann Sebastian Bach (1685-1750) to elaborate on its content and to expand its form to create new musical forms, the cantata and the Passion.

MUSIC IN ENGLAND

For geographical reasons, the composers of England worked alone and apart from the rest of the world. Music in England, like the music in the rest of Europe, was composed for the church or for the court. The preachings of Martin Luther spread to England with the formation of the Anglican Church or the Church of England. English composers continued to write Latin motets and Latin Masses but they also developed a new form suited to the needs of the Anglican Church, the *anthem*. The anthem was written in the imitative style (*polyphonic*) and set to an English text of a religious nature.

The rise of English secular music is directly connected to the Elizabethan Age. The most important secular vocal music of this time was the English *madrigal*. Madrigals are the songs written for small groups in which several voice parts are skillfully combined so that each part is interesting and independent both melodically and rhythmically. The madrigals are sung without instrumental accompaniment and are frequently based on a secular text or fable of the times.

FUNCTION OF MUSIC

Music played a very important part of life in the Renaissance. The well-educated man was expected to be an amateur musician who could read music and perform as an instrumentalist or as a singer. Every monarch in Europe was interested in music and many of them were good players or singers. The art of the period testifies to the fact that music literacy was not restricted to the aristocracy but was an important part of daily life. Many paintings illustrate the peasant or lowly shepherd with lute in hand enjoying music by singing. The Renaissance was a period of intense growth in the field of music, especially vocal music.

RENAISSANCE STYLE

From one point of view, the history of musical style could be seen as a constant battle between certain basic principles of musical composition: emphasis on the harmony of the music or emphasis on the melody of the music (homophony versus polyphony). The Renaissance period is identified as a period of intense growth in the melodic aspect of musical composition. Music of this period is primarily linear; that is, each part (for voices or instruments) is equally important, is melodically independent, and serves to reinforce the important melodies in the composition through imitation.

The Renaissance was a time in which a cappella music flourished. The term *a cappella* literally means "for the chapel." Although a cappella music was originally written for the church, today the term is interpreted as music which is performed by voices alone and is not restricted to sacred music only. The sixteenth century has come to be known as "the Golden Age of a cappella music."

The music of the Renaissance was written in imitative style; that is, one voice part sings out a vocal line which is then imitated by each of the other voice parts. The greatest composer of the imitative style was Giovanni Pierluigi da Palestrina (ca. 1525-1594) who was maestro di cappella at St. Peter's Cathedral in Rome. His music was the perfect example of order, restraint, balance, and good taste. Other composers imitated his style of composition and his music stood as the ideal model for other composers.

Because the emphasis in Renaissance music is on melody, the music has no strict rhythmic phrasing. It was not metered (there was no time signature and no barlines) and therefore the patterns of regular groupings of strong and weak beats did not exist. Renaissance music is governed by the musical organization of the melodic line which gives it a linear emphasis and weakens the groupings of beats.

Renaissance music is not bound to traditional rules of harmony. The harmony results from the sounding of the melodic lines in combination and is not ruled by order or function.

Renaissance vocal music is closely bound to the words; that is, the words determine the tempo, mood, dynamics, and musical phrasing of the composition. Renaissance composers did not use dynamic markings or tempo indications; first, because they usually prepared the performances of their own music and therefore could tell performers how they wanted their own music to be sung or played; second, because tempo and dynamic markings had not yet been invented; and third, because performance practices were generally understood by the performers.

The Baroque Period (1600-1750)

The term "Baroque" comes from the Portuguese word "barocca" meaning "an irregularly shaped pearl." It is a term borrowed from the fine arts to describe art that was considered (by Renaissance standards) to be "abnormal, bizarre, exaggerated, in bad taste, or grotesque." The art, sculpture, and architecture of this period are considered to be overly decorative, dramatic, flamboyant, and emotional. If Baroque music is compared to Renaissance standards of musical perfection (simplicity, balance, restraint, and refinement), these terms could also be applied to the music of the Baroque. The music is decorative in its use of trills and other forms of musical ornamentation; it is dramatic in its operas, oratorios, and cantatas; it is flamboyant in its attention to the virtuosity of the soloist; and it is emotional in that the moods are musically expressed (sorrow would have a slow-moving, drowsy melody broken with many sighs and happiness would be a fast-moving melody, probably in a major key).

TEXTURE

The move from the Renaissance to the Baroque brought about an important change in the texture of music. In Renaissance music, the melody is supreme, and all musical material comes from the inspiration of the melody. Baroque music centers its attention on the harmony and the function of the harmony. Basically, the change was from a linear or horizontal texture (polyphony) to a vertical texture (homophony). This is not to say that the melody lost its importance in Baroque music; on the contrary, the Baroque melody and the bass line formed the skeleton or outline of musical ideas which could be freely improvised by the performer. The *thoroughbass technique* (figured bass or continuo), as it was called, employed a kind of musical shorthand. The composer wrote a melody line and a bass line with numbers below the pitches of the bass line. These numbers would tell the performer what harmonies were intended by the composer, and the performer could fill in the harmonies himself. The melody was also slightly improvised through the practice of ornamentation.

HARMONY

The transition from the church modes (scales) of the Renaissance to the major-minor system of tonality was one of the most important changes in music history. With a major or minor key center, each chord has a function in relation to that key center. Composers of the Baroque period began to explore the movement from the home key to contrasting keys and back to the home key. This basic three-part harmonic structure led to the eventual shaping of musical forms such as the symphony.

RHYTHM

Rhythm in Baroque music takes on major importance. Music of this period has a strong feeling of forward motion. Unlike Renaissance music, Baroque music is metered and thus has regular groupings of strong and weak beats in each measure. For the first time in music history, composers wrote measured music, using time signatures and barlines. The tempo of the music did not change until the very end, thereby strengthening the basic pulse of the music.

DYNAMICS

Dynamic markings and expressive markings were practically unknown in Baroque music. Dynamic ranges were controlled by the number of players or singers who were asked to perform at one time. Small groups were contrasted with large groups to produce an effect of soft and loud or light and shade.

IMPORTANT VOCAL FORMS OF THE BAROQUE PERIOD

The most significant vocal form originating in the Baroque period was the dramatic opera. Opera began as dramatic entertainment for the nobility but gradually became public entertainment to be enjoyed by everyone. Opera evolved into two basic types: *opera seria* (serious or grand opera) and *opera buffa* (comic opera). Opera used a chorus, soloists, and orchestra, and a number of musical forms were developed for its dramatic and structural needs (recitative, aria, arioso, and chorus).

The religious parallel to opera was the *oratorio*, a musical composition with a religious text which is performed without scenery, costumes, or action, by solo voices, chorus, and orchestra.

The oratorio of the middle of the Baroque period was not much different from opera in that its major emphasis was on the solo singer. Not much emphasis was given to the chorus until George Frideric Handel (1685-1759) produced his oratorios in England. Handel dared to be different from other oratorio composers by moving the importance from the soloist to the chorus and by writing the text in English rather than in Latin or Italian as other composers had done. He wrote many important oratorios but his best known and most widely performed oratorio is *Messiah*.

The *cantata* was a sacred vocal form which developed in the Baroque period. It consisted of a number of movements or sections such as arias, recitatives, duets, and choruses. The cantata could be sacred or secular and was usually accompanied by orchestra. The sacred cantata was highly developed in Germany especially by Heinrich Schütz (1585-1672), Dietrich Buxtehude (ca. 1637-1707), and Johann Sebastian Bach (1685-1750). Bach's sacred cantatas (195 of about 300 have been preserved) open with a chorus in fugal style, move to recitatives and solo arias for the two or three soloists, and close with a chorale. All are in German and were written to correspond to the needs of the church year.

FUNCTION OF MUSIC

The Baroque era was a time of absolute governments in Europe; that is, countries were ruled by kings and queens, not by the people. Patronage of the arts continued but moved from a patronage by the Church to a patronage by the aristocracy and nobility. Many European courts were important in the development of musical culture in the Baroque period. Patrons of music included Popes, emperors, kings of England and Spain, rulers of smaller Italian and German states, churches, and the aristocrats of European cities and towns. Large courts, such as the one at Versailles, maintained an entire company of professional musicians and performers including an opera troupe, chapel choir, court orchestra, and of course a resident composer and conductor of all the musical events.

The Renaissance was dominated by sacred vocal music written for church use. Music of the Baroque period moved to the courts and was basically secular. The concentration also moved from vocal music to instrumental music. Again, the function of the music determined the change; that is, Renaissance music was mostly sacred and therefore primarily vocal. Baroque music was mostly secular, catering to the courtly functions of the aristocracy, threfore it was primarily instrumental.

Opera grew primarily as an independent form for the entertainment and pleasure of the aristocracy; ballet music came into being; and the courtly music in the form of chamber music and keyboard music developed new and important musical forms of composition.

The Classical Period (1750-1825)

The end of the Baroque period is marked by the year of Bach's death, 1750. In general, music of the Classical period is objective. It shows polish, refinement, balance, and lyricism, and is not overly emotional. It is the period when the various forms of music (especially instrumental forms) became clearly defined to serve as models for later composers. Like the Renaissance, it was a time when composers, writers, and artists turned to the masterpieces of the Greeks and Romans for their inspiration.

The Classical period witnessed the most complete development of the patronage system of the arts. Austria and Germany became the undisputed musical centers of Classical music activity. These countries were not governed by a single ruler and therefore still had many small courts which strongly supported the arts. Composers still depended upon the patronage of the courts or of the aristocratic society, but toward the end of the century, the nobility lost some of its wealth and power and could no longer support an entire community of artists and musicians. The concert hall and the opera house were made available to the general public and brought music to the people.

Through technical advances in music printing, music was readily available to amateur musicians. The public interest in music led to increased interest in the history, theory, and practice of music. Public performances were reviewed and critiqued, much as they are today. By the end of the century, music was in the hands of the general public.

CLASSICAL STYLE

One of the most important developments of music in the Classical period was the evolution of clearly defined musical forms. Classical composers organized their music into precise, clear, and well-balanced sections. The most popular formal organization developed from the contrast of two basic melodies, "Melody A" and "Melody B," which were equally balanced to an A-B-A structure. Audiences could easily identify both of the melodies which formed the basis for the development of musical ideas. Music of the Classical period is identified not only by the symmetry of its formal organization but also by the symmetry of its musical phrases.

MELODY

Classical composers placed strong emphasis on the importance of the melody. Classical melodies are generally lyrical and easily singable. The phrases are usually four measures in length. Elements of folk music were gradually introduced into serious music. Audiences could easily recognize familiar folk melodies and rhythms of composers such as Franz Joseph Haydn (1732-1809).

RHYTHM

Music of the Classical period uses simple and constant rhythmic patterns which serve to accompany the basic ingredient of the music, the melody. Tempos in Classical music are constant for an entire section and do not slow until the end of a section or a movement.

Silence (long rests) became part of the element of rhythm in Classical music. The ends of sections (*cadences*) are often followed by an entire measure of rest to clarify or strengthen the cadence.

HARMONY

Key signatures were firmly established in the Classical period. The harmony is strongly tonal and generally simple. Classical composers use harmony structurally; that is, there is a formal key relationship between the themes of the movements which helps to contrast the musical ideas.

MEDIA

Whereas the Renaissance was mainly a period of vocal music and vocal forms, the Classical period was a time for instrumental forms and instrumental music. Composers wrote music for orchestra, chamber orchestra, solo instruments with orchestra, or music for small groups of instruments. The Classical period was the first to organize the instruments of the orchestra into different groups or families: strings, woodwinds, brasses, and percussion. Each instrumental group was treated as an individual choir.

Instrumental music for small groups (chamber music) became very popular in the Classical period. Music became a performer's art and was widely enjoyed by the general public. Composers began to use expressive markings such as *forte* (loud) or *piano* (soft) to indicate their desires to the performers. Dynamic markings were used to build contrast into the music. Tempo markings were also indicated by the composers.

IMPORTANT COMPOSERS OF THE CLASSICAL PERIOD

The Classical period is represented by a very few, very important, highly respected, and most influential composers: Franz Joseph Haydn, Wolfgang Amadeus Mozart, and Ludwig van Beethoven. Haydn produced more music than any other composer of the Classical period (104 symphonies, 82 string quartets, 15 piano concertos, 60 piano sonatas, much chamber music for various combinations of instruments, 12 Masses, 3 oratorios, and about 20 miscellaneous works for choir). His entire professional career was in the service of an aristocrat and for thirty years he was the Court Composer and Conductor in the court of Prince Esterházy of Austria.

Wolfgang Amadeus Mozart (1756-1791), like Haydn, wrote a large quantity of music in a variety of forms. In his short life of only thirty-five years, Mozart wrote over 600 compositions. His music includes symphonies, concertos, chamber music, string quartets, operas, piano music, songs, Masses, a Requiem, and almost fifty miscellaneous pieces for choir.

The music of Ludwig van Beethoven marks the transition between the Classical and Romantic periods. His early works are Classical in style while the music of his later years is clearly Romantic. Most of his music was in the instrumental forms (9 symphonies, 11 overtures, a violin concerto and 5 piano concertos, 16 string quartets, 9 piano trios, 10 violin sonatas, 32 large piano sonatas) but he did write some important vocal music (one oratorio, one opera, and two Masses).

The Romantic Period (1800-1910)

The turn of the nineteenth century marks the beginning of a style of literature, art, and music known as Romantic. The nineteenth century was a time of drastic changes in culture and thought. The aristocratic society was fading and politics became a concern of every man. The French Revolution marked the end of an era in which the common man was ruled by the feudal-agricultural aristocracy. The middle class became the ruling class and the government was turned over to the people. Freedom (political, economic, religious, and personal) was the essence of the Romantic spirit.

The political freedom of the nineteenth century was carried over into artistic freedom in the arts. Poets, composers, writers, and artists created to satisfy themselves, not an employer. The Romantic period was the beginning of the self-employed artist. This freedom proved to be a mixed blessing. The artist was free to create works which were self-inspired, but then he had to sell his work in order to survive. The Romantic Age was a time of personal struggle for the artist. Many composers, artists, poets, and writers suffered intense poverty. They tended to withdraw from society and band together to draw inspiration from one another.

There was a real blending of the arts as had never existed before. Writers were very knowledgeable in the field of music; some were composers or performers. Likewise, composers were very interested in literature and in writing and some were important writers as well as composers. Composers such as Schubert, Schumann, and Wolf were inspired by the Romantic poets to produce an unequaled treasury of solo songs (Schubert wrote over 600 songs to the poetry of nineteenth-century poets).

The Romantic movement in the arts began in literature with Jean Jacques Rousseau (1712-1778) who rebelled against the intellectual, formal aspect of the Classical tradition and turned instead to the simple and natural, with an emphasis on man's feelings and instinct rather than on his intellect. Romantic music, poetry, and literature are very emotional and very personal. They center on the individual.

Music, as an emotionally expressive art, made it necessary for composers to use detailed expressive markings to tell the performers and conductors exactly how they wanted their music performed. An entire vocabulary of expressive terms emerged to tell not only the tempo but also the mood: "dolce" (sweetly), "cantabile" (in a singing manner), "maestoso" (majestically), "dolente" (weeping), "con passione" (with passion), "con fuoco" (with fire), and "con amore" (with love, tenderly).

Nationalism was an important influence in Romantic music. The composer used folk songs, folk dances, and legendary folk heroes to identify his music with his native land. National pride was woven into serious music. Each country produced music which reflected the character of that country and therefore was easily recognized as Spanish, Russian, Norwegian, or Finnish. Germany, Italy, England, and France had so long dominated the development of musical style that other countries wanted to establish their own musical traditions based on national elements.

CHARACTERISTICS OF STYLE

Music of the Romantic period was structured into the traditional forms developed in the Classical period, but the composer worked with greater freedom within the form. In addition, new forms were developed such as the nocturne and fantasy. The sections or movements are not symmetrical or balanced. Phrases are often organized into an uneven number of measures. Forms are not as precise or as predictable as in the Classical period.

MELODY, HARMONY, AND RHYTHM

In music of the nineteenth century, the basic ingredients of music (melody, rhythm, and harmony) are all emotionally inspired. The melody often grows out of the harmonies and is not as independent as the melody of the Classical period. Melodies are not organized into predictable phrases, and the length of the musical phrase varies. Rhythm is often irregular, more interesting, and changes frequently. Tempo is not constant in Romantic music. The composer freely alters the tempo with the use of accelerando and rubato. The Baroque period witnessed the evolution of the major-minor key structure; in the Romantic period the eventual breakdown of the tonal system began. Harmonies change frequently, are unpredictable, and use chromaticism to build harmonic tension.

MEDIA

The radical changes in the music of the nineteenth century were in part due to the Industrial Revolution which had a direct effect on the orchestras of the age. Instruments were mass-produced and so they were cheaper and more readily available. Instruments were greatly improved and performers could better realize the musical demands of the composer. The addition of valves to the brass instruments made it possible for performers to display virtuoso techniques of playing. The iron-cast frame and thicker strings on the piano turned it into an expressive solo instrument.

The gradual change from an aristocratic society to a democratic society brought music from the courts to the concert halls. Public concerts necessitated an increase in the size and capabilities of the orchestra. The acoustics and size of the hall demanded more flexibility in musical expression.

The Romantic period brought about the development of the virtuoso performer. Instruments had been perfected and therefore could allow the player more flexibility. The piano became the most popular instrument of the Romantic period. Through various technical advances, the piano was capable of a wide range of sound. It was especially popular because it could provide a complete musical experience and yet could be played by one person. In an age when the individual was the center of all developments it was especially appropriate to have a symbol of the expressive arts which could focus attention on the individual.

The orchestra was the preferred medium for composers of the nineteenth century. It was larger than the Classical orchestra and several instruments were added (clarinet, English horn, saxophone family, and several percussion instruments). The larger orchestra and the added instruments expanded the possibilities of sound and gave the composer more variety in tone color.

The choral music of the nineteenth century falls into three main categories:

1. Part songs or short choral pieces in which the composer uses the chorus as the main ingredient. Songs are performed either a cappella or accompanied by piano or organ.
2. Music with religious texts which are written for use in the church.
3. Music for chorus and orchestra (with or without soloists) which is intended to be performed in a concert hall.

The Twentieth Century

Throughout the long history of music, changes in style and practice occurred which evolved over a long period of time. It took many hundreds of years to develop our present system of musical notation, to evolve into a major-minor system of tonality, to refine musical forms, and to develop professional skills as a performer. In less than 100 years, the twentieth century has gone through changes in attitude and expression that make the previous musical revolutions seem minor. Each composer's search for individuality has led to new and different forms of musical expression. Composers of the twentieth century believed that the basic ingredients of music (pitch, melody, harmony, rhythm, and tone color) had been explored to their limits by previous composers and it was now time to find new ways to express themselves. The following is a brief listing of some of the more common compositional techniques used by composers in the twentieth century.

PITCH

The basic twelve tones of the octave have been divided into quarter tones (24 pitches to the octave), and eighth tones (48 different pitches to the octave). This technique is called *micro-tonality* and requires a new form of musical notation and very exceptional performers in order to be realized. Instrumentalists must technically adjust pitches to perform music that is micro-tonal. Singers and instrumentalists must have unusually discriminating ears to be able to adjust the scale into quarter tones and eighth tones.

MELODY

Generally speaking, the melodies of twentieth-century composers are shaped in angles rather than in curves; that is, they employ wide intervals which move suddenly between high and low pitches. They are often written to explore the extreme ranges of the instrument or voice. In addition, twentieth-century melodies are usually very complicated rhythmically.

HARMONY

Twentieth-century harmonies are more freely dissonant. Composers use dissonance not as a means of building tension but as a part of the basic harmonic makeup of the music. Some composers create dissonance by writing music that uses two different key centers at the same time (*bitonality* or *poly-tonality*). Twentieth-century harmony is unpredictable and is therefore exciting. The listener cannot predict the direction of the harmony of twentieth-century music.

RHYTHM

Generally speaking, the rhythm of twentieth-century music is more complicated than that of its predecessors. Twentieth-century composers change the meter frequently and often alternate simple and compound meters. In addition, they often use meters that are of odd-numbered metric patterns (5/4, 7/8, 11/8, etc.). Twentieth-century music is marked by a great deal of variety in the rhythm. Composers often like to emphasize the rhythm over the melody or harmony.

EXPRESSIVE MARKINGS

Composers of the twentieth century are usually very specific as to how their music is to be played or sung. The tempo indication is usually given in words to identify the mood and in metronomic markings to identify the precise speed of the notes. Individual parts are very precisely marked with appropriate dynamic markings or mood indications. The traditional Italian terms are often written in the composer's native language. The twentieth-century composer communicates directly with the performer regarding his desires for a proper rendition of his music.

TEXT

The text to which the music is written is directly and intimately woven into the music. There is a direct attempt to communicate with the audience and the listener.

FUNCTION OF MUSIC

The technological advancements of the twentieth century have had a great impact on music. Radio, the movies, and television have placed great demand on the composer for incidental music.

Music in any form is available to everyone—at the supermarket, in the dentist's chair, the home, the car, at the office, or at the beach. Through advancements in sophisticated recording techniques, music is easily reproduced and can be acoustically adjusted to suit individual taste. Musical research has enlightened our knowledge of the music of the past. Musicians are better trained than ever before, and the quality of excellence of the professional musician has steadily increased until only the true virtuoso can make a living in serious music.

An entirely new kind of musician has emerged, the arranger of folk songs, popular songs, religious songs, Christmas carols, etc., for the steady and growing needs of the amateur choir. Sales of music by music publishers have become a very large industry. Schools, civic organizations, colleges and universities, churches, semi-professional and professional organizations have provided the music publishers with a ready market.

Today's composers are well-trained, imaginative, daring, and highly individualistic. Each has his/her own style which may or may not be consistent with the style of previous efforts. We, the consumers or performers, must approach the music of the twentieth century with the same sense of wonder and discovery that was felt by the composer at the time of its creation.

Vocal Production

THE VOICE

Just as physical appearance varies from one individual to the next, so does the sound of the speaking and singing voice. Each individual's voice is unique, because of physical characteristics and the way the voice is used.

The efficiency of the human voice as a sound producer is unparalleled. No man-made sound-producing device can equal the capacity of the human voice to communicate ideas and to express feelings.

It is appropriate to regard the voice as a sound-producing "machine," and to think of the singing voice as an instrument. Although each individual's voice has a characteristic quality, it is important to be aware of the role proper use of the voice plays in determining how effective and expressive each person's voice can become as a communicator.

The singing process is triggered by a mental command to activate a complex series of physical actions which will convey the singer's concept of how the text set to music should sound. After inhaling, the good singer utilizes controlled, active physical involvement to control the flow of air into the lungs and through the vocal cords in the larynx. The vibrations which result from this flow of air pass through the resonating cavities of the chest and head, creating a distinctive tone color. Tones become intelligible sounds when the mouth and tongue are shaped to direct the flow of air to produce specific vowel and consonant sounds.

As he sings, the vocalist is concerned with the pitch, length, and volume of each note of his part. He is also responsible for the clarity of each word, achieving precise attacks and releases, and reproducing a tone quality appropriate to the music.

When an individual does not maintain the mental concentration and physical control necessary to produce a good singing tone, vocal problems such as the following may occur:

harsh quality — caused by constricted, or tense muscles in the throat area.

nasal quality — caused by failure to utilize the vocal resonators in the proper manner.

breathy quality — literally, there is more breath than tone, because extra air is allowed to pass between the vocal cords.

Learning to use the voice as an expressive musical instrument is a challenge which involves both mental and physical effort.

THE CHORAL REHEARSAL

Every rehearsal of a music group is a unique experience. It is important to make the most of each opportunity to work toward a standard of excellence. Repetition in a rehearsal should be viewed as an opportunity for each choir member to learn how to fulfill the demands of music being rehearsed.

The level of achievement of an individual singer or of a choir is directly related to the level of skills attained. Since a choir is made up of individuals, it can be only as good as each member is willing to make it. The dedication of each choir member to good vocal production is a key to choral success. Just as athletes must train their bodies to be competitive in a sport, so singers should train their bodies in order to excel as singers.

SINGING POSTURE

Just as a bent musical instrument cannot sound its best, so a singer cannot produce his best sounds with the body out of alignment. At all times when singing, the singer's posture should remain erect with the spine in a straight line. *Fight gravity*, which will pull the singer into a slump. The shoulders should be slightly back and down. If sitting during singing, keep the legs uncrossed and sit on the edge of a chair.

Exercise 1: Raising the chest. While standing, completely extend the arms above the head. Then lower the arms and shoulders, but allow the chest to remain in its high position. The shoulders should remain down. The shoulder blades will feel as if they are slightly pulled together in the back. This is correct. Maintain this posture at all times while singing, whether sitting or standing.

BREATHING

Breathing is a natural activity. Breathing to sing requires special concentration so that the singer can sustain pitches, achieve musical phrasing, and provide dynamic contrasts. Following is a description of what happens when you breathe to sing.

When the chest is in its proper, erect position, the ribs and the front part of the abdomen are then free to move back and forth to allow for deep breathing. On inhalation, the ribs (front and back) and the front part of the abdomen should expand, just as a balloon moves out as it is filled. As the rib muscles relax and expand the ribs, the diaphragm (a circular, somewhat flat muscle which separates the chest cavity from the lower abdomen) tenses and flattens. These two movements enlarge the chest cavity, creating a vacuum and allowing the lungs to fill.

These are a singer's checks for proper breathing:
1. The area at the waist should expand.
2. The chest should not rise.

Exercise 2: Place one hand on the front part of the body, just below the waist. Place the other hand on the chest. Inhale slowly through the nose, allowing the hand on the abdomen to move out, away from the body. The hand on the chest should not rise and the shoulders should not rise. Exhale slowly—observe that the hand on the abdomen area will move in toward the body as the singer exhales.

THE RAISED SOFT PALATE

The correct singing position of the inside of the mouth is the feeling of the beginning of a "yawn—sigh." The singer who has this sensation should also have a raised soft palate (velum) and an enlarged pharynx (back of the mouth). Be careful not to yawn fully. This will cause the swallowing muscles to tense, creating a strident sound. Be sure that the tip of the tongue touches the base of the bottom front teeth during all sustained vowel sounds (forward tongue placement).

EXERCISES TO ACHIEVE A RAISED SOFT PALATE

No. 1: With the mouth open, take a quick, deep breath as if in surprise. The cold spot in the back of the mouth is the soft-palate area. With this type of breath, the palate will usually rise.

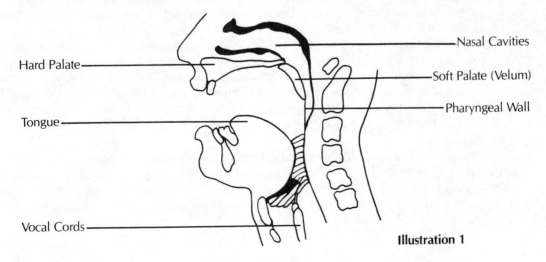

Hard Palate

Tongue

Vocal Cords

Nasal Cavities

Soft Palate (Velum)

Pharyngeal Wall

Illustration 1

No. 2: With the mouth closed, begin to yawn with the jaw dropped (always back, not protruding). This will produce the feeling of an enlarged pharynx or open throat (see Illustration 1).

BENEFITS OF SINGING WITH AN OPEN THROAT (RAISED SOFT PALATE)

1. To extend pitch and dynamic range with less tension than would be experienced otherwise.
2. To increase vocal stamina, permitting the singer to sing for longer periods of time without tiring.
3. To make singing more beautiful because tension is decreased and extra resonating areas in the head are opened.
4. To increase pitch control, since large skips tend to be under pitch if the palate is lowered.

HEAD TONE

The entire body is actually a vocal resonator. However, most resonation should take place in the mouth, pharynx, and nasal passages. During initial, quiet exercises, the singer should imagine that the tone is coming from the area around the eyes and upper cheekbones. The following exercises are designed to improve the quality of sound by helping to direct the vocal sound waves into the various resonating chambers, especially in the head. These exercises should at first be done at a mezzo piano level. Always avoid pushing the sound. It is especially important that the soft palate be raised at all times.

Exercise 1: A well-produced hum aids in establishing a head tone. It should be produced with the jaw down and the lips barely touching. As the pitch ascends, be sure that the inside of the mouth remains open, the soft palate raised, and the jaw down. Strive to transfer the quality of the hum into the "ah" sound.

Hum_____ ah_____ Hum_____ ah_____

Continue up by half steps.

VOCAL QUALITIES IN YOUNG VOICES

Since a singer has only one voice to last a lifetime, there are several things he should remember to preserve his voice and develop his talent. Young voices have unique characteristics. Problems with changing ranges of pitches which can be easily reproduced and uncertainty in tonal production may last only days for some singers and may last several months for others. The key-word is patience. Using good vocal habits will lessen the ordeal of the "change." Both girls and boys can expect to encounter some vocal changes as their voices develop. Vocal range may be limited at times. The singer should strive to sing where it is comfortable and be patient as his range is gradually extended. At the first sign of strain or hoarseness, the singer should exercise caution. Good physical habits may lessen the strain. Adequate rest and good physical health contribute to good vocal health. Cheerleading can cause severe vocal problems, and great care should be used when cheering, even as a spectator. Singing too loudly or trying to sing beyond the limits of range can cause vocal strain.

Establishing a falsetto in all young male voices is an important step toward achieving vocal control of both high and low tones. It is possible, as the falsetto is used and strengthened, to mix it into the full voice, thus permitting a full range of dynamics throughout the vocal range. Remember to strive to carry the quality of the upper tones into the lower ones and to avoid pushing for loud sound at either end of the vocal range.

26

Exercise 2: Mixing falsetto in the lower range. Descend as smoothly as possible. Do not be concerned if there is a break in the sound at some point in the exercise as the singer moves from head voice to full voice. Begin with the throat open and maintain a raised soft palate throughout the exercise.

Continue up by half steps until as high as comfortable.

Popular recording artists often use a technique of tone production commonly known as "the chest voice." This approach to producing tone can cause much of the upper head resonance of female singers to be lost. In choral singing, this type of production may contribute to intonation problems as well as adversely affecting blend and balance. The recommendation that boys working with falsetto should strive for a naturally light, unforced sound applies to young altos and sopranos as well. If the sound produced seems forced or is unusually loud, it may be an indication of chest voice. As young women begin to utilitze the head voice, chest resonance will begin to mix with the sound, bringing about an increase in richness and fullness over a period of time. Allowing the voice to develop naturally is a process which calls for patience. It cannot be hurried.

In summary, remember that singing is a *natural* activity. If at any time strain or discomfort occurs, the singer should ask:

1. Is the head level and is the chin down (not protruding)?
2. Is the head properly aligned so that the jaw is in singing position?
3. Is forward tongue placement being employed?
4. Is the face relaxed?
5. Is the tone free and unforced?
6. Is the feeling of a suppressed ("half") yawn maintained so that the throat is open?

THE CHORAL WARM-UP

A good choral warm-up leads to the production of a good choral tone. Though each choir has a unique and distinctive sound, certain general rules apply. Just as an athlete must warm up to perform well, so must a singer. There are three types of warm-ups for singers:

1. Mental: The singer's attitude must be one of dedication to improving his own vocal habits through concentration on the physical aspects of singing.

2. Physical: The body must be prepared to sing. Simple exercises should be done before singing.
   a. Head rolls: Slowly revolve the head in as wide a circle as is comfortable.
   b. Stretch: Reach over your head and stretch the muscles along your sides. Continue the stretch as you twist from side to side. Lower your arms and continue to twist.

3. Vocal: It is important to begin the vocal warm-up quietly, but with energy and concentration. In the beginning of the warm-up, the singer should concentrate on allowing tones to resonate quietly and freely in the front part of the face. This area is sometimes called the "mask" of the face. The term "forward focus" is often used in reference to this type of tone placement. Keep the jaw relaxed and moving freely, being careful that it does not protrude. The quality of head tones should be carried into the lower range. Avoid loud, harsh tones, especially in the lower part of the voice. As an aid to achieving freedom in tone production, the singer might imagine the tone "spinning" or "swirling" with quiet energy.

28

Music for Mixed Chorus

1. ECCE QUAM BONUM

(SEE HOW GOOD, HOW RIGHT)

Psalm 133
Adapted by M.K.

Jean Richafort
Edited by Maynard Klein

31

32

2. O BELLA FUSA

(THE SPINNING WHEEL)
(Canzonetta)

English text by M.K.

Orlando di Lasso
Edited by Maynard Klein

mo que - ste fu, que - ste fu, que - ste fu -s'in pro -
come, come and buy, Come and buy, come and buy, see it

mo que - ste fu, que - ste fu, que - ste fu -s'in pro -
come, come and buy, Come and buy, come and buy, see it

mo que - ste fu, que - ste fu, que - ste fu -s'in pro -
come, come and buy, Come and buy, come and buy, see it

mo que - ste fu, que - ste fu, que - ste fu -s'in pro -
come, come and buy, Come and buy, come and buy, see it

36

va. Noi le ven - di - mo que - ste fu, que - ste fu, que - ste
go! Will some-one please come, come and buy? Come and buy, see it

va. Noi le ven - di - mo que - ste fu, que - ste fu, que - ste
go! Will some-one please come, come and buy? Come and buy, see it

va. Noi le ven - di - mo que - ste fu, que - ste fu, que - ste
go! Will some-one please come, come and buy? Come and buy, see it

va. Noi le ven - di - mo que - ste fu, que - ste fu, que - ste
go! Will some-one please come, come and buy? Come and buy, see it

3. IL PIACERE

(JOY FOR ALL, GIVE US PLEASURE)

(Balletto)

English adaption by M.K.

Giacomo Gastoldi
Edited by Maynard Klein

40

From "Ballets for five voices with verses for singing, playing and dancing". Published in Venice, 1591. To be sung with high spirit and feeling of fun.

42

4. CHI LA GAGLIARDA

(COME DANCE THE GALLIARD)

(Villanella)*

English text by M.K.

Baldassare Donato
Edited by Maynard Klein

* A light-hearted Neopolitan madrigal
\> indicates phrase rhythm

The Galliard is a dance in three-in-a measure rhythm with rapid complex steps. It was of Italian origin. The name suggests gaiety.

la Ga - gliar - da, don - ne, vo'im-pa - ra -
dance the gal - liard, maid - ens, come now have

gliar - da, don - ne, vo'im - pa - ra -
gal - liard, maid - ens, come now have

44

gliar - da don - ne, vo'im-pa - ra -
gal - liard, maid - ens, come now have

gliar - da, don - ne, vo'im-pa - ra -
gal - liard, maid - ens, come now have

re, Chi la Ga - gliar - da, chi
fun, Come dance the gal - liard, come

re, Chi la Ga - gliar - da chi la Ga -
fun, Come dance the gal - liard, come dance the

re, Chi la Ga - gliar - da, chi la Ga -
fun, Come dance the gal - liard, come dance the

re, Chi la Ga - gliar - da, chi la Ga -
fun, Come dance the gal - liard, come dance the

46

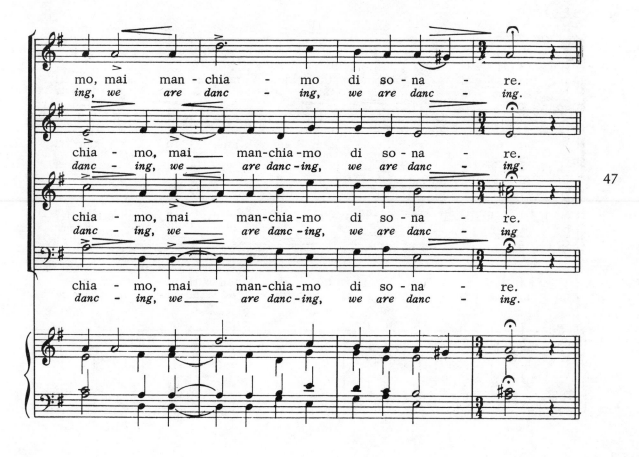

47

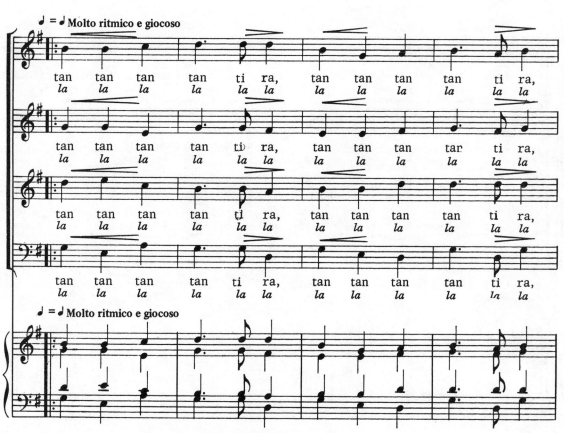

48

5. GLORIA PATRI
(GLORY TO GOD)

English text by George Mead

Giovanni Pierluigi da Palestrina
Edited by Frank Damrosch

53

54

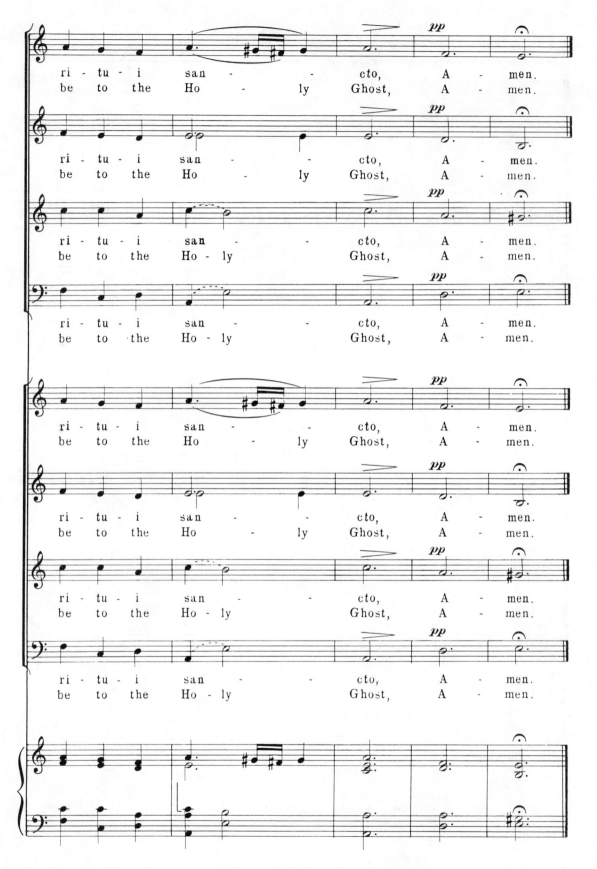

6. POPULE MEUS
(TELL ME, MY PEOPLE)

Liber usualis
English version by John Colman

Tomás Luis de Victoria
Edited by Clifford Richter

55

Tempo mark, dynamic, and expression marks are editorial additions; the original contains none. Accidentals in parenthesis are cautionary.

* Although this work was written for two antiphonal choirs, it can be sung by one choir; the contrasts can be effected by observing the suggested dynamics.

56

7. SPRINGTIME MANTLETH EV'RY BOUGH

Thomas Morley
Arranged and edited by Walter Barrie

58

60

8. JESU, JOY OF MAN'S DESIRING

(Chorale from Church Cantata No. 147)

Johann Sebastian Bach
Arranged by Bryceson Treharne

61

SOPRANO
Je - su, joy of man's de - sir - ing,
Wohl mir, dass ich Je - sum ha - be,
Through the way where hope is guid - ing,
Je - sus blei - bet mei - ne Freu - de,

ALTO
man's de - sir - ing,
Je - sum ha - be,
hope is guid - ing,
mei - ne Freu - de,

62

TENOR
Je - su, joy of man's de - sir - ing,
Wohl mir, dass ich Je - sum ha - be,
Through the way where hope is guid - ing,
Je - sus blei - bet mei - ne Freu - de,

BASS

Ho - ly wis - dom, Love most
o wie fe - ste halt' ich
Hark, what peace - ful mu - sic
mei - nes Her - zens Trost und

Ho - ly wis - dom, Love most
o wie fe - ste halt' ich
Hark, what peace - ful mu - sic
mei - nes Her - zens Trost und

Love most
halt' ich
mu - sic
Trost und

Word of God, our flesh _____ that
Je - sum hab' ich, der _____ mich
Theirs is beau - ty's fair - - est
mei - ner Au - gen Lust _____ und

Word of God, - our flesh _____ that
Je - sum hab' ich, der _____ mich
Theirs is beau - ty's fair - - est
mei - ner Au - gen Lust _____ und

67

round_ Thy ____ throne.
Her - ze ____ bricht.
joys_ un - known.
und_ Ge - sicht.

68

round_ Thy ____ throne.
Her - ze ____ bricht.
joys_ un - known.
und_ Ge - sicht.

9. THE HEAVENS ARE TELLING

(from: The Creation)

English translation by
Robert Shaw and Alice Parker

Joseph Haydn

Gabriel *(Soprano Solo)*

Re-veal'd are His ways by day__ un-to

Uriel *(Tenor Solo)*

Re-veal'd are His ways by day un-to

Raphael *(Bass Solo)*

Re-veal'd are His ways__ by__ day__ un-to

71

sotto voce

day, By night that is

sotto voce

day, By night that is

sotto voce

day, By night that is

gone to fol - low-ing night, By night that is gone to

gone to fol - low-ing night, By night that is gone to

gone to fol - low-ing night, By night that is gone to

72

73

tongue be dumb, ne-ver, ne-ver, ne - ver,— ne ver

tongue be dumb, ne-ver, ne-ver, ne - ver, ne - ver

tongue be dumb, ne-ver, ne-ver, ne - ver, ne - ver

Più Allegro

tongue be dumb.

tongue be dumb.

tongue be dumb.

Più Allegro

The hea - vens are tell - ing the glo - ry of

The hea - vens are tell - ing the glo - ry of

The hea - vens are tell - ing the glo - ry of God; With

The hea - vens are tell - ing the glo - ry of God; With

Più Allegro

God; With won-ders of His work, with won-ders of His work re-

God; With won-ders of His_work re-sounds, re-

won - ders, with won-ders of His_work re-sounds, re-

won-ders, with won-ders of His work, with won-ders of His work re-

fz *fz*

77

sounds the_fir-ma-ment,

sounds the fir-ma-ment,

sounds the fir-ma-ment,

sounds the fir-ma-ment,

ment, the fir-ma-ment, With

sounds the fir-ma-ment, With won-ders of His work re-

With won-ders of His work re-sounds the fir-ma-

With won-ders of His work re-sounds, re-sounds the fir-ma-

79

won-ders of His work re-sounds the fir-ma-ment, the fir-ma-

sounds the fir-ma-ment,

ment, With won-ders of His work re-sounds the fir-ma-

ment, With won-ders of His work, with won-ders of His

re - sounds,___ re - sounds___ the_ fir - ma - ment,   With won-ders

ment,   With won-ders of His work___ re -

___ re - sounds___ the fir - ma - ment,   With_ won - ders re -

With won-ders of His work re - sounds the fir - ma -

of His work re - sounds the fir - ma - ment,   With

sounds,   re - sounds the fir - ma - ment,   With

sounds the fir - ma - ment, the fir - ma - ment,

ment,_____ the fir - ma - ment,   With

won-ders of His work, with won-ders of His work re-

won-ders of His work, with won-ders of His work re-

82

With won-ders of His work re-sounds the fir - ma-

won-ders of His work, with won-ders of His work re-

fz

sounds, re - sounds the ___ fir - ma-ment. The

sounds, re - sounds the ___ fir - ma-ment.

ment, the fir - ma - ment. The hea - vens are

sounds, re - sounds the fir - ma - ment. The ___

f

84

sounds, re-sounds the___ fir - ma - ment. The

sounds, re-sounds the___ fir - ma - ment.

ment, the fir - ma - ment. The hea - vens are

sounds, re-sounds the fir - ma - ment. The___

85

hea - vens are tell - ing the glo - ry of God; With

The hea - vens are tell - ing, are

tell - ing the glo - ry of God;_____

hea - vens are tell - ing the___ glo - ry of God;_____

86

ment, re - sounds the fir - ma - ment, re - sounds the fir-ma-

work re - sounds the fir - ma - ment, re - sounds the fir-ma-

_ re - sounds the fir - ma - ment, re - sounds the fir-ma-

sounds the fir - ma ment, re - sounds the fir-ma-

ment, re - sounds the fir - ma - ment.

ment, re - sounds the fir - ma - ment.

ment, re - sounds the fir - ma - ment.

ment, re - sounds the fir - ma - ment.

10. AVE, VERUM CORPUS
(HAIL, TRUE BODY)

English text by A.K.

Camille Saint-Saëns
Arranged by Abraham Kaplan

89

90

For David Slater

11. THE SILVER SWAN

Anonymous (c. 1612)

Diana Abraham

92

sung her first ___ and _ last and sung no more.

___ si - lent throat.

lightly

Soprano   Poco Adagio

mp

The sil - ver

Alto   *mp cantabile*

The sil - ver swan, who ___

Tenor, Bass   *mp cantabile*

The sil - ver swan, who ___

Poco Adagio

mp legato

swan had no note, When ___ death ___ ap -

liv-ing had no note, When death ap - proached ___ un-locked her si - lent throat

liv-ing had no note, When death ap - proached ___ un-locked her si - lent throat

-proached___ un - locked___ her___ si -

Lean-ing her breast a - gainst the reed-y shore. Thus sang her first

Lean-ing her breast a - gainst the reed-y shore. Thus sang her first

- - lent throat.

and_ last and sang no more.

and_ last and sang no more.

Andante (with more spirit)

94

More geese than swans now live, More fools— than wise.

More geese than swans now live, More fools— than wise.

95

Fare - well, all joys; O death, come close mine eyes. More

Fare - well, all joys; O death, come close mine eyes. More

Fare - well, all joys; O death, come close mine eyes. More

mf

geese than swans now live, More fools than wise.

geese than swans now live, More fools__ than wise.

geese than swans now live, More fools__ than wise.

96

A tempo - sadly

Sil - ver swan who liv - ing had no note,

A tempo

12. SPRING CAROL

L.A.C.

Larry A. Christiansen

SOPRANO
1. Cool the stream,
2. Scarce - ly heard,

ALTO
Hum

TENOR
Hum

BASS
Hum ____ Hum

Piano
(for rehearsal only)

gen - tle the breez-es, flow'rs fresh and fra - grant fill the fields.
songs soft and gen - tle, sooth - ing the songs_the lark does sing.

99

13. THIS IS A GREAT COUNTRY

Theron Kirk

great coun-try, the land where ev-'ry-one is free. This is a

This is a

great coun-try, a great coun-try, a land of op-por-tu-ni-

great coun-try, a great coun-try, a land of op-por-tu-ni-

ty for all, A great coun-try, a great coun-try, the

ty for all, A great coun-try, a great coun-try, the

103

104

land of prom-ise, a land where dreams come true. This is a

land of prom-ise, a land where dreams come true. This is a

105

land of beau-ty, a land of prom-ise, a land where dreams come

land of beau-ty, a land of prom-ise, a land where dreams come

true. This is a great coun-try, a great coun-try, a

true. This is a great coun-try, a great coun-try, a

14. THE LORD BLESS YOU AND KEEP YOU

Peter Lutkin
Arranged by William Stickles

*May be sung unaccompanied.

108

gra - cious un - to you, be gra - cious, The Lord be

and be gra-cious, and be gra-cious, The Lord be

and be gra-cious, and be gra-cious, The Lord be

and be gra-cious, and be gra - cious, The Lord be

gra-cious, gra - cious un - to you.

gra-cious, gra - cious un - to you.

gra-cious, gra - cious un - to you. A - men, A -

gra-cious, gra - cious un - to you. A - men, A -

15. THE SHEPHERD'S CHORUS

(from: Amahl and the Night Visitors)

Words and music by
Gian Carlo Menotti

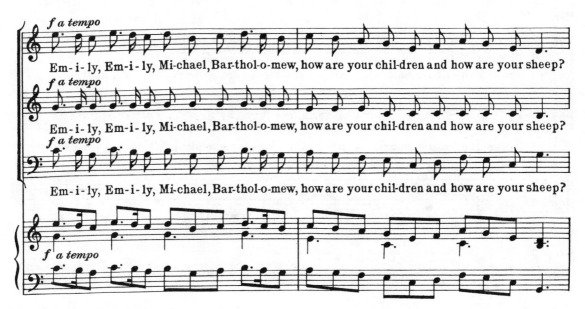

Also published for S. A. T. B.

112

Dor-o-thy, Dor-o-thy, Pe-ter, E-van-ge-line, give me your hand, come a-long with me.

Dor-o-thy, Dor-o-thy, Pe-ter, E-van-ge-line, give me your hand, come a-long with me.

Dor-o-thy, Dor-o-thy, Pe-ter, E-van-ge-line, give me your hand, come a-long with me.

senza staccati

All the chil-dren have mumps, All the flocks are a-sleep. We are go-ing with A-

senza staccati

All the chil-dren have mumps, All the flocks are a-sleep. We are go-ing with A-

div. *unis.* *senza staccati*

All the chil-dren have mumps, All the flocks are a-sleep. We are go-ing with A-

mahl,   bring-ing gifts to the Kings. Ben-ja-min, Ben-ja-min, Lu-cas, E-liz-a-beth,

mahl, — bring-ing gifts to the Kings. Ben-ja-min, Ben-ja-min, Lu-cas, E-liz-a-beth,

mahl,   bring-ing gifts to the Kings. Ben-ja-min, Ben-ja-min, Lu-cas, E-liz-a-beth,

how are your chil-dren and how are your sheep? Car-o-lyn, Car-o-lyn, Mat-thew, Ver-on-i-ca,

how are your chil-dren and how are your sheep? Car-o-lyn, Car-o-lyn, Mat-thew, Ver-on-i-ca,

how are your chil-dren and how are your sheep? Car-o-lyn, Car-o-lyn, Mat-thew, Ver-on-i-ca,

Solo Soprano

Ah,

Kath-er-ine, Kath-er-ine, Chris-to-pher, Ba-bi-la, how are your chil-dren and how are your sheep?

Kath-er-ine, Kath-er-ine, Chris-to-pher, Ba-bi-la, how are your chil-dren and how are your sheep?

unis.

Kath-er-ine, Kath-er-ine, Chris-to-pher, Ba-bi-la, how are your chil-dren and how are your sheep?

115

come ____ a-long _ with me.

div.

Jo-seph-ine, Jo-seph-ine, An-ge-la, Jer-e-my, come ____ a-long _ with me.

Jo-seph-ine, Jo-seph-ine, An-ge-la, Jer-e-my, come ____ a-long _ with me.

Jo-seph-ine, Jo-seph-ine, An-ge-la, Jer-e-my, come_ a-long ____ with me.

117

Thank you, thank you, thank you kind- ly. Thank you, thank you,

Thank you, thank you, thank you kind- ly. Thank you, thank you,

Thank you, thank you, thank you kind- ly. Thank you, thank you,

119

thank you kind-ly.

thank you kind-ly.

thank you kind-ly.

Ha-zel-nuts and cam-o-mile, mignon-ettes and laur - el,

Ha-zel-nuts and cam-o-mile, mignon-ettes and laur - el,

l. h.

hon-ey-combs and cin-na-mon, thyme, mint and gar - lic, this is all we

hon-ey-combs and cin-na-mon, thyme, mint and gar - lic, this is all we

this is all we

shep-herds can of - fer you. Take them, eat them, you are wel-come.

shep-herds can of - fer you. Take them, eat them, you are wel-come.

shep-herds can of - fer you. Take them, eat them, you are wel-come.

Take them, eat them, you are wel-come, too!

Take them, eat them, you are wel-come, too!

Take them, eat them, you are wel-come, too!

Bass Solo (Balthazar)

liberamente

Thank you, good friends, for your danc - es and your gifts. But

now we must bid you good night. We have lit-tle time for sleep and a long jour-ney a-head.

121

122

bright. Good night, good night. The dawn is in sight. Good night, fare-well, good night, good

bright. Good night, good night. The dawn is in sight. Good night, fare-well, good night, good

bright.　　　Good night, good night. The day will be bright. Good night, fare-well, good

night.

night.

night.

123

16. I LOST MY LOVE IN SCARLET-TOWN

(from: The Lowland Sea)

Arnold Sundgaard

Alec Wilder
Arranged by John Sacco

124

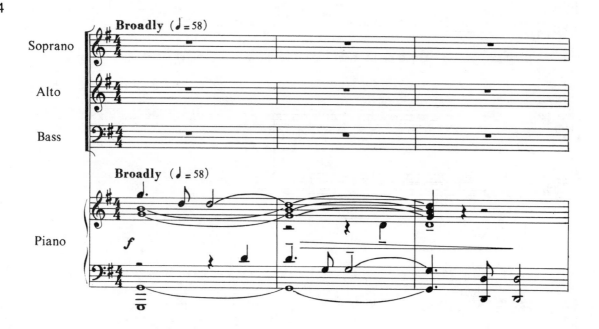

Where blows the wind when the wind blows cold? Where it blows

Where blows the wind when the wind blows cold? Where it blows

Where blows the wind when the wind blows cold? Where it blows

Also published for S.A.T.B.

125

126

Sing - a - pore, I nev - er saw John-ny Dee no more.

Sing - a - pore, I nev - er saw John-ny Dee no_more.

mf Solo Soprano

Oh! Scar - let - town, oh, Scar - let - town, I

(All) *p*

Where blows the wind when the wind blows cold?

(All) *p*

Where blows the wind when the wind blows cold?

(All) *p*

Where blows the wind when the wind blows cold?

128

cruised a - way for__ Sing - a - pore. I nev - er saw John-ny

Where blows the wind when the wind blows free? It blows my true love

Where blows the wind when the wind blows free? It blows my true love

Where blows the wind when the wind blows free? It blows my true love

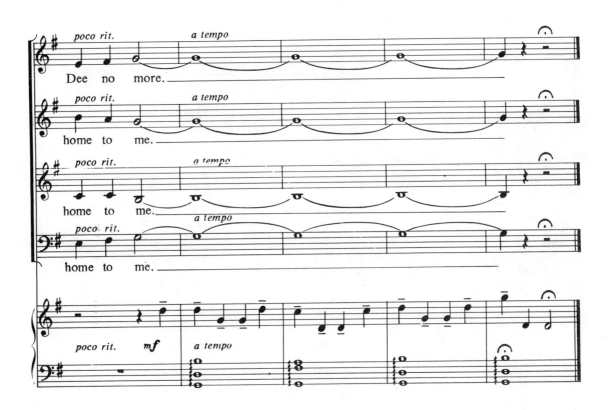

Dee no more.__

home to me.__

home to me.__

home to me.__

17. GREAT DAY!

Traditional

Spiritual
Edited and arranged by Walter Ehret

130

*Some second altos may sing with tenors.

131

132

133

call for val - iant heart - ed men,_ God's gon - na build up,

God's gon - na build up,

God's gon - na build up,

God's_ gon - na build up Zi -

God's gon - na build up,

on's walls,_____

walls,_ build_ Zi - on's_ walls._____

18. NINE HUNDRED MILES FROM HOME

Appalachian Mountain Folksong
Arranged by Emile Schillio

135

eyes,   Tryin' to read a let-ter from my home;_____

_____ If that train's a-run-ning right, I'll be home to-mor-row

night, 'Cause I'm nine hun - dred miles___ from my home,___

night, 'Cause I'm nine hun - dred miles___ from my home,___

night, 'Cause I'm nine hun - dred miles___ from my home,___

night, 'Cause I'm nine hun - dred miles___ from my home,___

___ And I hate to hear that lone - some whis - tle blow.___

hate to hear that lone - some whis - tle blow.___

___ And I hate to hear that lone - some whis - tle blow.___

___ hate to hear that lone - some whis - tle blow.___

138

(Solo or Soli)
mf

I will

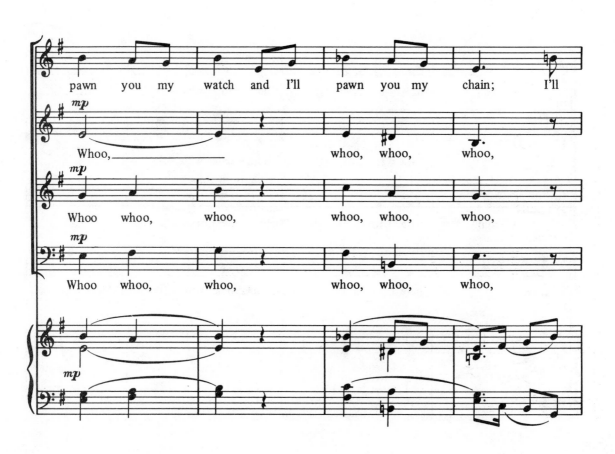

pawn you my watch and I'll pawn you my chain; I'll

mp
Whoo,_____ whoo, whoo, whoo,

mp
Whoo whoo, whoo, whoo, whoo, whoo,

mp
Whoo whoo, whoo, whoo, whoo, whoo,

mp

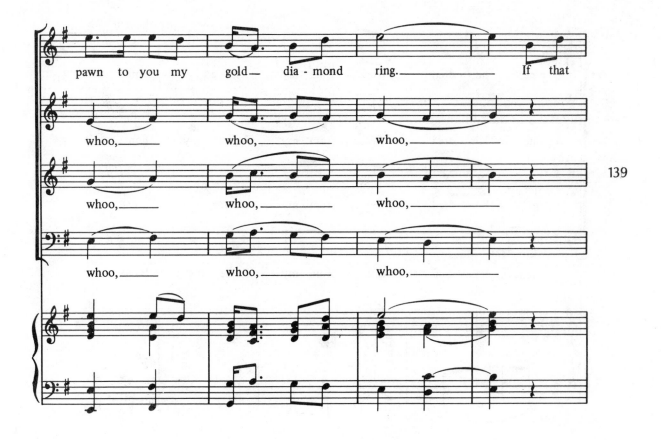

pawn to you my gold— dia - mond ring._____ If that

whoo,_____ whoo,_____ whoo,_____

whoo, whoo, whoo,

whoo,_____ whoo,_____ whoo,

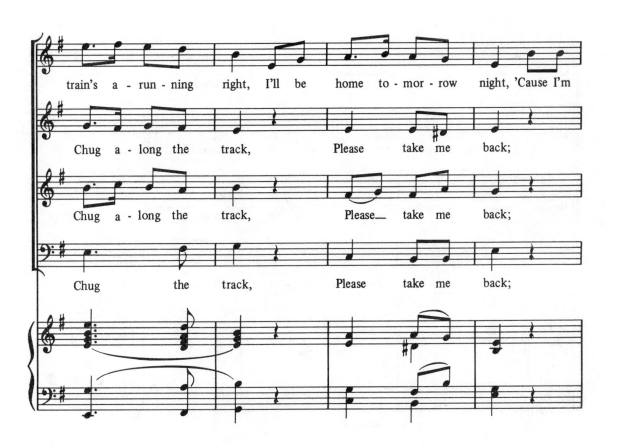

train's a - run - ning right, I'll be home to - mor - row night, 'Cause I'm

Chug a - long the track, Please take me back;

Chug a - long the track, Please— take me back;

Chug the track, Please take me back;

140

nine hun-dred miles____ from my home, home, And I

nine hun-dred miles____ from my home, my home, And I

nine hun-dred miles____ from my home, home,

nine____ hun-dred miles from my home, my home,

go, lone-some whis-tle blow._____

hate to hear that lone-some whis-tle blow._____

go, lone-some whis-tle blow._____

go, lone-some whis-tle blow._____

più mosso

141

142

nine hun-dred miles___from my home._____ And I

nine hun-dred miles___from my home, sweet home, And I

nine___ hun-dred miles___from my home, sweet home, And I

nine hun-dred miles___from my home, sweet home, And I

hate to hear that lone-some whis-tle blow far from home.

hate to hear that lone-some whis-tle blow far from home.

hate to hear that lone-some whis-tle blow far from home.

hate to hear that lone-some whis-tle blow far from home.

rall.

19. SCARBOROUGH FAIR

(With Piano, String Bass or Guitar, Cymbal and Bass Drum)

English Folk Song
Arranged by Margaret Vance

144

145

146

doo doo, Then she'll be a true love of mine.

doo, Then she'll be a true love of mine.

doo, Then she'll be a true love of mine.

work, Then she'll be a true love of mine.

147

mf

A   Dm   G   Am   Dm   G7

Love im - pos - es im -

Love im - pos - es im -

Love im - pos - es im -

Love im - pos - es im -

sim.

F7   E♭7   Am7   Dm   G   Dm   G9

148

pos - si - ble tasks, Pars - ley, sage, rose - mar - y and thyme.

pos - si - ble tasks, Pars - ley, sage, rose - mar - y and thyme.

pos - si - ble tasks, Pars - ley, sage, rose - mar - y and thyme.

pos - si - ble tasks, Pars - ley, sage, rose - mar - y and thyme.

Dm7   F   Bb   Am   G9   A7

ff   mf

Though not more_____ than an - y heart asks_____ one to be a

Though not more_____ than an - y heart asks_____ one to be a

Though not more_____ than an - y heart asks_____ one to be a

Though not more_____ than an - y heart asks_____ one to be a

Dm   Gm   A   Dm   G7

149

20. SLUMBER SONG OF THE CHILD JESUS

(With Wind and Percussion Accompaniment)

Old French Noel
Arranged by Janice Kneer

150

Close to the ox and don-key mild, Sleep, sleep, sleep my lit-tle child. Heav'n-ly cher-u-bim, hosts of ser-a phim,

* *Suggested Instruments: Resonator, bells, glockenspiel, recorders, flutes, or Orff instruments*

Hov-er all a - round the lit-tle Lord of Love.

Soprano

Mild li -lies white and ro - ses red,

Alto

Lil - ies white and ro - ses red,

152

Sleep, sleep, in Thy low-ly bed. Heav'n-ly cher-u-

Sleep my lit-tle ba-by in Thy_ low-ly bed._

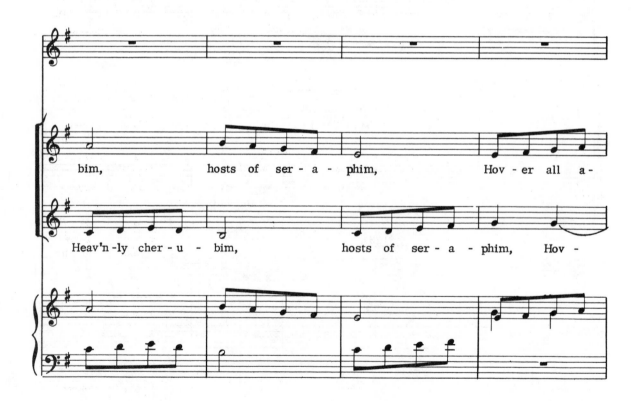

bim, hosts of ser-a-phim, Hov-er all a-

Heav'n-ly cher-u-bim, hosts of ser-a-phim, Hov-

round the lit -tle Lord of Love.

- er round Lord of Love.

153

Soprano

Close to the ox and don - key mild, sleep,

Alto

Close to the ox and don - key

Tenor

Close to the

154

MUSIC FOR MIXED CHORUS
Analyses and Texts

The following outlines are intended as reference materials for the music included in this volume, rather than complete theoretical analyses.

The outlines are presented with the hope that both teachers and students may utilize them as points of departure for further study as the music is rehearsed.

1. ECCE QUAM BONUM / Jean Richafort (ca. 1480-1548)
(See How Good, How Right)   (edited: Maynard Klein)

Form:	A B C
	(A m. 1 / B m. 11 / C m. 24)
Tonality:	G major
Metric Elements:	A and B - 3 / pulse in one 4
	C - 4 / pulse in two 4
Texture:	polyphonic canonic/imitation between soprano and tenor and alto and bass parts melismatic treatment of melodic lines for jucundum and alleluia four voices SATB / a cappella
Text:	Latin and English

Ecce quam bonum,	**Literal Translation**
et quam jucundum	Behold, how good
habitare fratres in unum.	And pleasant it is
Alleluia.	For brethren to live in unity.
Psalm 133: adapted by Maynard Klein	

2. O BELLA FUSA / Orlando di Lasso (1532-1584)
(The Spinning Wheel)   (edited: Maynard Klein)

Form:	canzonetta / AA BB C DD
Tonality:	AA (m. 1 and m. 10) - D major / half-cadence on dominant A at end of section
	BB (m. 19 and m. 25) - D major / cadence on dominant of the dominant, E major triad
	C (m. 31) - D major
	DD (m. 38 and m. 43) - D major but with suggestion of G major
Metric Elements:	¢ meter / emphasis on syllabic stress rather than bar lines

Texture:	chordal
	four voices SATB / a cappella

Text:	Italian and English

O bella fusa; chi no vo accatare?
Noi le vendimo queste fus'in prova.
Son fu, son fusa nova.
Voi le provare.
Veni tell'a pigliare!
le dam' in prova.

English singing text: Maynard Klein

Literal Translation
Oh beautiful spindle,
Who wants to borrow it?
We could sell this spindle,
this spindle on approval.
Make the spindle whirl,
make the new spindle whirl!
For you to test it
I came to try the cloth,
to test the ladies.

157

3. IL PIACERE / Giacomo Gastoldi (1556-1622)
(Joy for all, give us pleasure)   (edited: Maynard Klein)

Form:	balletto / ABB (with fa-la-la refrain)

Tonality:	constantly moving between C major and a harmonic minor / final cadence A major (Picardy third)

Metric Elements:	A - 3 meter / pulse in one
	4
	B - C meter / pulse in two

Texture:	chordal
	five voices SSATB / a cappella

Text:	Italian and English

Al piacer, a la gioia,
Con noi ognum sia intento
Se vuol esser contento.
Fa la la . . . . .

English singing text: Maynard Klein

Literal Translation
On pleasure,
On joy,
May each of us be intent,
If one if is to be satisfied.
Fa la la . . .

4. CHI LA GAGLIARDA / Baldassare Donato (ca. 1530-1603)
(Come dance the Galliard)   (edited: Maynard Klein)

Form:	villanella / AA B CC
	(A m.1 and m. 7 / B m. 13 / C m. 29 with repeat)

Tonality:	A - G major
	B - basically G major / cadence on dominant of the dominant, A major triad
	C - G major

Metric Elements:	A B - ₵ meter
	C - 3 / pulse in one
	4
	strong rhythmic pulse emphasizes the dance-like quality of the music

Texture:	polyphonic
	A - voices enter at different times ABTS
	B C - basically chordal
	four voices SATB / a cappella

| **Text:** | Italian and English |

Chi la Gaghiarda, donne, vo'imparare,
Venite a noi che siamo mastri fini,
Che di sera e di mattina,
 mai manchiamo di sonare.
Tan tan tan tan ti ra.

English singing text: Maynard Klein

Literal Translation
Anyone who wants
to learn the gailliard, ladies,
come to us
we are masters at it,
who in the evening and the morning
never fail to dance it.
tan tan tan tan tira, etc.

5. GLORIA PATRI / Giovanni Pierluigi da Palestrina (ca. 1525-1594)
 (Glory to God)   (edited: Frank Damrosch)

| **Form:** | two sections denoted by the text |

| **Tonality:** | basically F major |
| | m. 24 cadence in d minor / at m. 27 movement toward a minor begins / final cadence on dominant of a minor |

| **Metric Elements:** | 3 meter / pulse in one |
| | 4 |

| **Texture:** | chordal / sung antiphonally by two choirs |
| | four voices SATB / a cappella |

| **Text:** | Latin and English |

Gloria patri et filio,
 et spiritui sancto,
Amen.

English text: George Mead

Literal Translation
Glory be to the Father,
the son, and the
Holy Ghost,
Amen.

6. POPULE MEUS / Tomás Luis de Victoria (1548-1611)
(Tell Me, My People)   (edited: Clifford Richter)

Form: A B C
                     (A m. 1 / B m. 15 / C m. 29)

Tonality: Basically F major

Metric Elements: C / pulse in slow two

Texture: basically chordal / antiphonal / limited canonic style entrances in C section
                     four voices SATB / a cappella

Text: Latin and English

Popule meus, quid fecit tibi?
 aut in quo contristavi te?
 responde mihi.
Agios, o Theos.
Sanctus Deus.
Agios ischyros.
Sanctus fortis.
Agios athanatos, eleison imas.
Sanctus et immortalis, miserere nobis.

Literal Translation
Oh my people,
What have I done to thee?
And where have I wearied thee?
Answer me.

Agios, o Theos,
Holy God.
Agios ischyros.
Holy and strong.
Agios athanatos,
eleison imas.
Holy and immortal,
Have mercy upon us.

English singing text: John Colman

7. SPRINGTIME MANTLETH EV'RY BOUGH / Thomas Morley (1557-1603)
(arranged: Walter Barrie)

Form: madrigal / A B with repeats / example of English ballett, characterized by
                     the fa-la-la refrain

Tonality: D major

Metric Elements: 4 meter / pulse in two
                     4

Texture: triadic
                     three voices SAB / a cappella

Text: English

8. JESU, JOY OF MAN'S DESIRING / Johann Sebastian Bach (1685-1750)
(from Church Cantata No. 147)   (arranged: Bryceson Treharne)

Form: two stanzas

the music of the first two phrases of the chorale is exactly repeated at A / starting at B two phrases of the chorale follow in sequence / a slightly modified version of the first two phrases recurs at C

the phrases of the chorale are interrupted and enhanced by the keyboard accompaniment

Tonality: G major

Metric Elements: $\frac{3}{4}$ meter / characterized by triplet figure

in the accompaniment contrasting with slower chorale movement in voices

Texture: homophonic
triadic/ornamented by numerous passing tones
four voices SATB / organ accompaniment

Text: English and German

Stanza 1
Wohl mir, dass ich Jesum habe,
 o wie feste halt'ich ihn,
 dass er mir mein Herze labe,
 wenn ich krank und traurig bin.
Jesum hab'ich, der mich liebet
 und sich mir zu eigen giebet,
 ach drum lass'ich Jesum nicht,
 wenn mir gleich mein Herze bricht.

Stanza 2
Jesus bleibet meine Freude,
 meines Herzens Trost und Saft,
Jesus wehret allem Leide,
 er ist meines Lebens Kraft,
 meiner Augen Lust und Sonne,
 meiner Seele Schatz und Wonne,
 darum lass'ich Jesum nicht!
 aus dem Herzen und Gesicht.

Literal Translation
It is well for me that I have Jesus,
Oh how tightly I hold Him,
that He may refresh my heart.
When I am sick and sorrowful,
I have Jesus, who loves me,
And Himself unto me for my own gives.
Ah therefore I do not leave Jesus,
Even if my heart breaks.

Jesus remains my joy,
The comfort and sap of my heart,
Jesus restrains suffering for all,
He is my life's strength.
My eyes' desire and sun,
My soul's treasure and delight.
Therefore I do not let Jesus
Out of my heart and sight.

9. THE HEAVENS ARE TELLING / Franz Joseph Haydn (1732-1809)
(from *The Creation*)

Form: A B C D D' E Coda
(A m. 1 / B m. 23 / C m. 38 / D m. 57 / D' m. 74 / E m. 95 / Coda m. 175)

Tonality: Basically C major

Metric Elements:	₵ meter

Texture:	A B C D chordal
	E canonic style
	A C E and Coda repeated text
	four voices SATB / soprano, tenor, bass solos / keyboard accompaniment /
	ornamentation contributes to the graceful quality of the music

Text:	English translation by Robert Shaw and Alice Parker

10. AVE, VERUM CORPUS / Camille Saint-Saëns (1835-1921)
   (Hail, True Body)   (arranged: Abraham Kaplan)

Form:	A B A′
	(A m. 1 / B m. 17 / A′ m. 33)

Tonality:	basically b harmonic minor
	B section utilizes altered tones to suggest other tonalities
	final cadence B major triad (Picardy third)

Metric Elements:	4 meter / pulse in two to create flowing movement
	4

Texture:	chordal
	four voices SATB / a cappella

Text:	Latin and English

Ave, verum Corpus natum de Maria Virgine:
  vere passum, in cruce pro homine:
Cujus latus perforatum,
  fluxit aqua et sanguine.
Esto nobis praegustatum mortis in examine.
O Jesu pie!
Tu nobis miserere.

Literal Translation
Hail, true Body,
born of the Virgin Mary:
You Who have truly suffered
on the cross for mankind:
From whose pierced side
flowed water and blood,
Be for us a provider
In the hour of death.
Blessed Jesus,
Have mercy on us.

English singing text: Abraham Kaplan

11. THE SILVER SWAN / Diana Abraham

Form:	A A′ B C B
	(A m. 5 / A′ m. 23 / B m. 40 / C m. 45 / B m. 61)

Tonality:	A B - e natural minor
	C - E major

Metric Elements: 2 meter / two measures each of 3 and 4 at cadences for text considerations
4   4   4

two rhythmic patterns in the accompaniment serve as a unifying force:

and

Texture:
A - two voices / SA with melody / TB with accompanying part
A' - three voices / ATB with melody of A section / S with descant
B - one voice / S with short transitory sentence
C - three voices / ATB with new melody, then joined by S, beginning in unison and ending the section in four parts SATB
B - beginning with S / ending in four parts SATB
SATB / piano accompaniment

Text: Anonymous (ca. 1612)

12. SPRING CAROL / Larry A. Christiansen

Form: strophic / introduction, two stanzas, refrain, coda

Tonality: F major

Metric Elements: 3 meter / pulse in one
4

Texture: homophonic / in stanzas one and two S has melody / ATB have humming accompaniment / in refrain, all parts sing words
four voices SATB / piano accompaniment

Text: Larry A. Christiansen

13. THIS IS A GREAT COUNTRY / Theron Kirk

Form:
A A' B B A' C D A²
A and its two variations serve as the unifying force
(A m. 6 / A' m. 14 / B m. 22 and 26 / A' m. 30 /
  C m. 38 / D m. 46 / A² m. 54)

Tonality:
A B C - F major
D - basically F major / limited use of accidentals for harmonic interest

Metric Elements: 4 meter
4
rhythmic pattern used throughout

Texture:	homophonic
	extended use of unison and two-voiced
	passages / limited use of four voices
	SATB / piano accompaniment

Texture: homophonic
extended use of unison and two-voiced
  passages / limited use of four voices
SATB / piano accompaniment

Text: Theron Kirk

14. THE LORD BLESS YOU AND KEEP YOU / Peter Lutkin (1858-1931)
(arranged: William Stickles)

Form: through-composed

Tonality: basically C major / accidentals give momentary suggestions
  of new tonalities

Metric Elements: $\frac{4}{4}$ meter / pulse in two

Texture: homophonic
chordal / limited canonic treatment in final section (Amen)
four voices SATB / optional keyboard accompaniment

15. THE SHEPHERD'S CHORUS / Gian Carlo Menotti
(from *Amahl and the Night Visitors*)

Form: through-composed
sectionalized by the text, which is characterized by dialogue between the
  chorus and the solo voices

Tonality: first section - C major
second section - B$\flat$ major
third section - E$\flat$ major / final chord and keyboard accompaniment ending
  G major

Metric Elements: first section - $\frac{12}{8}$ meter / pulse in four

second section - shifting meter $\frac{4}{4}$ $\frac{6}{8}$ $\frac{5}{8}$ $\frac{4}{4}$

third section - $\frac{12}{8}$ $\frac{6}{8}$

Texture: homophonic
three solo voices in unison / one voice (Balthazar) in short solo passage
three voices / SAB / solo voices TBB and S / divided soprano parts in last
  section / piano accompaniment

Text: Gian Carlo Menotti

16. I LOST MY LOVE IN SCARLET-TOWN / Alec Wilder (1907-1980)
   (from *The Lowland Sea*)   (arranged: John Sacco)

Form:	A B C
	(A m. 4 / B m. 19 / C m. 33)
Tonality:	G major
Metric Elements:	4 meter
	4
Texture:	A - chordal / SAB
	B - two solo voices / SA
	C - combination of A and B / soprano solo and choir
	three voices SAB / two solo voices / piano accompaniment
Text:	Arnold Sundgaard

17. GREAT DAY / Spiritual
   (arranged and edited: Walter Ehret)

Form:	A B C - each section based upon identical melody and text
	(A m. 3 / B m. 19 / C m. 35)
Tonality:	A - E$^\flat$ major
	B - E major
	C - F major
Metric Elements:	¢ / extensive use of syncopation
Texture:	homophonic
	four voices SATB / piano accompaniment

18. NINE HUNDRED MILES FROM HOME / Appalachian Mountain Folksong
   (arranged: Emile Schillio)

Form:	A B A′
	(A m. 5 / B m. 29 / C m. 54)
Tonality:	A B - e melodic minor
	A′ - f melodic minor
Metric Elements:	2 meter
	4
Texture:	homophonic
	four voices SATB / optional solo or soli / piano accompaniment

19. SCARBOROUGH FAIR / English Folk Song
  (arranged: Margaret Vance)

Form: A A′ B
                        (A m. 9 / A′ m. 28 / B m. 49)

Tonality: dorian mode / chromaticism, especially in TB, suggests d harmonic minor /
                          ending in dissonant harmony   165

Metric Elements: 3 meter / pulse in one
                        4

Texture: homophonic
                        A A′ - four voices SATB
                        B - limited occurrence of divided soprano parts
                        SATB / piano accompaniment / also string bass or guitar,
                          cymbal, bass drum

20. SLUMBER SONG OF THE CHILD JESUS / Old French Noel
  (arranged: Janice Kneer)

Form: A B A′ / based upon a single melody / A and A′ have same text
                        (A m. 9 / B m. 29 / A′ m. 48)

Tonality: e harmonic minor

Metric Elements: 2 meter
                        4

Texture: A - unison
                        B - two parts SA
                        A′ - three parts SAB (or SATB) / round for SSA, SAB, or SATB
                        piano for rehearsal / instrumental accompaniment included

Music for Treble Chorus

21. HODIE CHRISTUS NATUS EST

(ON THIS DAY CHRIST IS BORN)

English by M.K.

Claudio Monteverdi
Edited by Maynard Klein

172

174

in ex - cel - sis De - o, al - le - lu - ia,
be to God___ in the high - est, al - le - lu - ia,

ex - cel - sis De - o, al - le - lu - ia, al - le -
to God in the high - est, al - le - lu - ia, al - le -

De - o,___ al - le - lu -
high - est,___ al - le - lu -

al - le - lu - ia, al - le - lu - ia.
al - le - lu - ia, al - le - lu - ia.

- lu - ia, al - le - lu - ia, al - le - lu - ia.
- lu - ia, al - le - lu - ia, al - le - lu - ia.

ia, al - le - lu - ia, al - le - lu - ia.
ia, al - le - lu - ia, al - le - lu - ia.

22. LO, HOW A ROSE E'ER BLOOMING

English version by Theodore Baker

Michael Praetorius
Arranged by David Shand

176

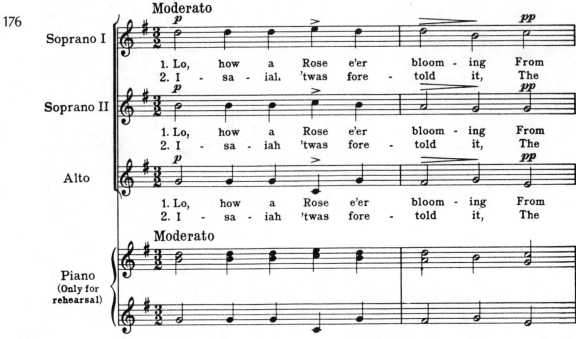

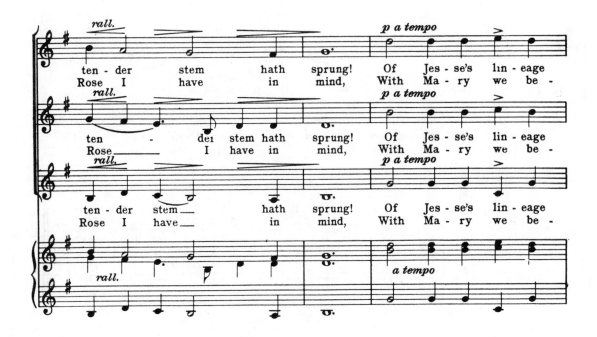

23. I WILL EXTOL THEE, MY GOD

Psalm 145:1, 3, 9

Georg Friedrich Handel
Arranged by Robert S. Hines

178

179

180

24. SING ALOUD TO GOD
(EFFUDERUNT SANGUINEM)

English text by R.G.P.

Michael Haydn
Edited by Reinhard G. Pauly

182

with a song be-fore Him. All the world____ shall pro-
to - rum tu - o - rum, qui ef - fu - sus, ef -

with a song be-fore Him. All the world shall pro-
to - rum tu - o - rum, qui ef - fu - sus, ef -

with a song be-fore Him. All the world shall pro-
to - rum tu - o - rum, qui ef - fu - sus, ef -

claim__His__great-ness, His great mer - cy.
fu - sus - est,____ su - per ter - ram,

claim__His__great-ness, His great mer - cy.
fu - sus - est,____ su - per ter - ram,

claim His great-ness, His great mer - cy.
fu - sus - est, su - per ter - ram,

14

186

all   the world shall pro-claim His great-ness,   His   great
qui   ef - fu - sus, ef - fu - sus - est ___   su - per

all   the world shall pro-claim His great-ness,   His   great
qui   ef - fu - sus, ef - fu - sus - est ___   su - per

all   the world shall pro-claim His great-ness,   His   great
qui   ef - fu - sus, ef - fu - sus - est   su - per

25

mer - cy.   Sing a - loud to   God, the God of Ja-cob!
ter - ram.   Ef - fu - de - runt   san - gui-nem sanc-to-rum,

mer - cy.   Sing a - loud to   God, the God of Ja-cob!
ter - ram.   Ef - fu - de - runt   san - gui-nem sanc-to-rum,

mer - cy.   Sing a - loud to   God, the God of Ja-cob!
ter - ram.   Ef - fu - de - runt   san - gui-nem sanc-to-rum,

25

187

lift up your hearts to the liv - ing God, come with a song be-fore Him.
vin-di - ca, do - mi-ne san - gui-nem sanc - to - rum tu - o - rum

190

lift up your hearts to the liv - ing God, come with a song be-fore Him.
vin-di - ca, do - mi-ne san - gui-nem sanc - to - rum tu - o - rum

lift up your hearts to the liv - ing God, come with a song be-fore Him.
vin-di - ca, do - mi-ne san - gui-nem sanc - to - rum tu - o - rum

All the world shall pro - claim_His_ good-ness, His great
qui ef - fu - sus, ef - fu - sus_ est___ su - per

All the world shall pro - claim_His_ good-ness, His great
qui ef - fu - sus, ef - fu - sus_ est___ su - per

All the world shall pro-claim His good-ness, His great
qui ef - fu - sus, ef - fu - sus est su - per

46

mercy, His great mercy. Sing a-loud to God; Sing
ter - ram, su - per ter - ram, qui ef-fu - sus est su-

mercy, His great mercy. Sing a-loud to God;
ter - ram, su - per ter - ram, qui ef-fu - sus est

mercy, His great mercy. Sing a-loud to God;
ter - ram, su - per ter - ram, qui ef-fu - sus est

___ a-loud to Him, sing a - loud to Him.
- per ter - ram, su-per ter - ram.

Sing a-loud to Him, sing a - loud to Him.
su -per ter - ram, su-per ter - ram.

Sing a-loud to Him, sing a - loud to Him.
su-per ter - ram, su-per ter - ram.

25. BE MERRY AND WISE

(Rounds for 3-5 Equal Voices)

From Apollonian Harmony, Vol. II (ca. 1790)

Edited by Jerome Gries

Now we are Met Let Mirth Abound

Samuel Webbe

192

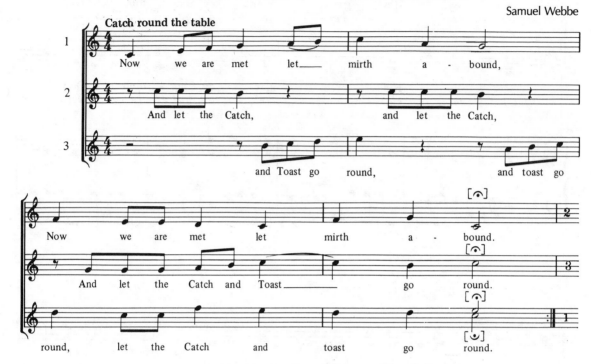

Pretty Maidens

Luffman Atterbury

Mister Speaker

Joseph Baildon

193

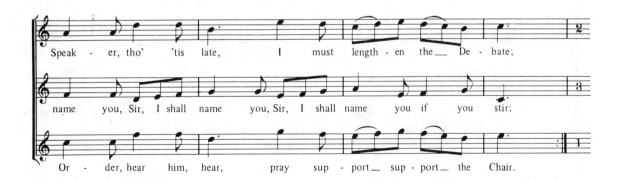

Do, Re, Mi, Fa, So, La

Anonymous

194

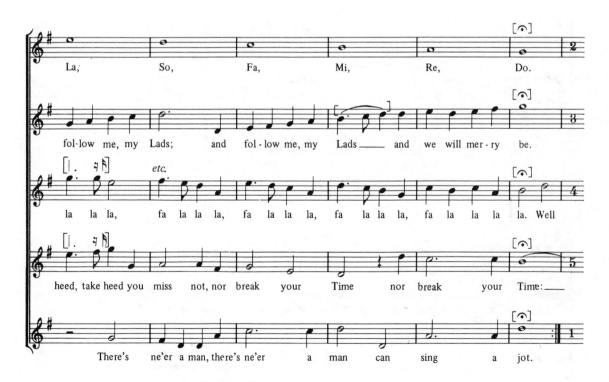

*C in original. **"Ut" in original.

I've Lost My Mistress, Horse and Wife

Dr. Samuel Green

195

* Originally a minor third higher.

Let Us be Merry in Our Old Cloaths

E. Gregory

Sir, You are a Comical Fellow

William Bates

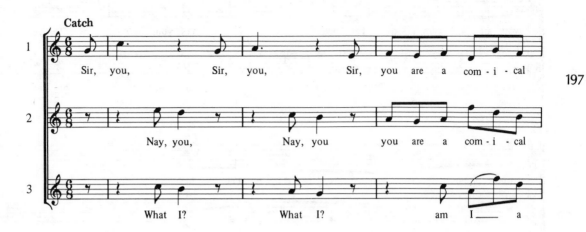

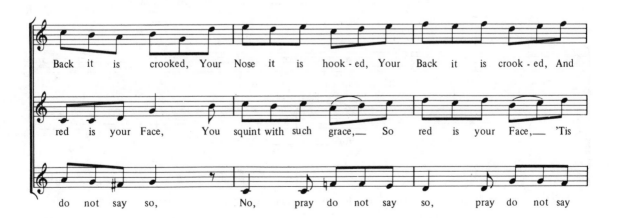

198

Wilt Thou Lend Me Thy Mare

Dr. James Nares

Here's a Health

Anonymous

Round

1. Here's a Health to all them that we love,

2. Here's a Health to all them that love us,

3. Here's a Health to all them that love those that love them,

4. love those that love them that love us.

199

'Tis Hum-Drum!

Henry Har(r)ington

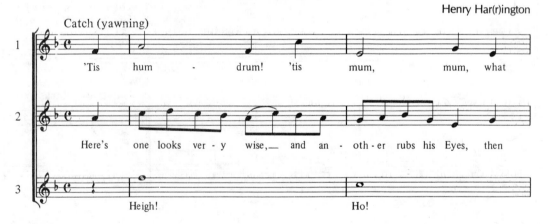

Catch (yawning)

1. 'Tis hum - drum! 'tis mum, mum, what

2. Here's one looks ver - y wise,— and an - oth - er rubs his Eyes, then

3. Heigh! Ho!

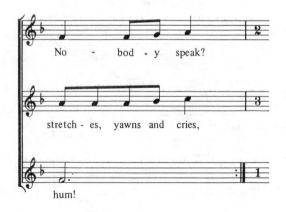

No - bod - y speak?

stretch - es, yawns and cries,

hum!

26. PRAYER from HANSEL AND GRETEL

Stanza 1 translated by Constance Bache
(from the German form of the White Paternoster)
Stanza 2 adapted by Willis Wager
(from the English forms of the same folk-prayer)

Engelbert Humperdinck
Arranged by Bryceson Treharne

200

SOPRANO

1. When at night I
2. Mat-thew, Mark, and

ALTO

1. When at night I
2. Mat-thew, Mark, and

go to sleep, Four-teen an - gels watch do keep: ___
Luke, and John, Bless the bed that I lie ___ on. ___

go to sleep, ___ Four-teen an - gels watch do ___ keep: ___
Luke, and John, ___ Bless the bed that I lie ___ on. ___

Two my head are guard - ing,
Bless - ed guard-ian an - gel,
Two my feet are
Keep me from all

Two my head are guard - ing,
Bless - ed guard-ian an - gel,
Two my feet are
Keep me from all

guid - ing,
dan - ger.
Two are on my right hand,
Now I fain would rest me,

guid - ing,
dan - ger.
Two are on my right hand,
Now I fain would rest me,

Two are on my left hand,
May the Lord now bless me.
Two who warm - ly
If I do not

Two are on my left hand,
May the Lord now bless me.
Two who
If I

202

203

27. NOW'S THE TIME TO SING

(With Descant Solo, Piano Four-Hands, and Percussion)

Theron Kirk

205

Now's the time to

sing; it's a bright new day!

Voice 2

Sing a song of joy; Sing a song of cheer!

206

Now's the time to sing; it's a bright new day!

Sing, sing with joy for this fine day!

207

209

La   la la la la la la, Sing a song of cheer!

Sing a song of joy;   Sing a song of cheer!

Sing   a song of love and peace.

Come join___ the song;   Sing out a hap-py tune!

8 -

Bb   Cm7   F   Bb

210

La la la la la la la la, La la la la la la la la,

Sing, oh, sing! Sing with a heart full of love.

Sing, sing with joy for this fine day!

Now's the time to sing; it's a bright new day!

211

La   la   la   la la la   la,   Sing   a   song   of cheer!

212   Sing   a   song   of   love   and   peace.

Come   join___ the   song;   Sing out   a hap - py   tune!

Sing a song of   joy;   Sing a song of   cheer!

8

B♭   Cm7   F   B♭

La la__ la la la la la la, La la__ la la la la la la,

Now's the time to sing, Now's the time to sing,

Sing, sing__ with joy, Sing, sing__ with joy,

Sing, oh, sing, Sing, oh, sing,

8

B♭   E♭   B♭   E♭

La la___ la la la la la la,   Sing a song of

214

Now's the time to sing,   Sing a song of

Sing,   sing___ with joy,   Sing a song of

Sing,   oh,   sing!   Sing a song of

joy! _____

joy! _____

215

joy! _____

joy! _____

(both Hands 8va)

B♭

28. FREE TO BE . . . YOU AND ME

(from: Free to Be . . . You and Me)

Bruce Hart

Stephen Lawrence
Arranged by Margaret Vance

To this land,_____ from where we are._____ Take my

To this land,_____ from where we are._____

hand. Come with me,_____ Where the chil - - dren are free._

Won't you come with me_____ Where we

Come with me,_____ take my hand_____ And we'll live...

all are free?_ Come with me, take my hand,

Voice I

_____ In a land_____ Where the riv-ers run

Voice 2

We'll find a place that's free In a land_____ Where the riv-ers run

Opt. Alto

In a land_____ Where the riv-ers run

free, In a land_____ Through the green coun - try, In a land__

free, In a land_____ Through the green coun - try, In a land__

free, In a land_____ Through the green coun - try, In a land__

221

222

try, To a land____ to a shin-ing sea,____ To a land___

try, To a land____ to a shin-ing sea,____ To a land__

try, To a land____ to a shin-ing sea,____ To a land__

____ Where the chil-dren are free, And you and me____ Are free to be__

____ Where the chil-dren are free, And you and me____ Free to be__

____ Where the chil-dren are free, You and me____ Free to be__

29. GOOD NIGHT, LITTLE JESUS

R.E.P.

Robert E. Page

225

Slowly, but with rhythm

Good night, lit-tle Je-sus, good night. The

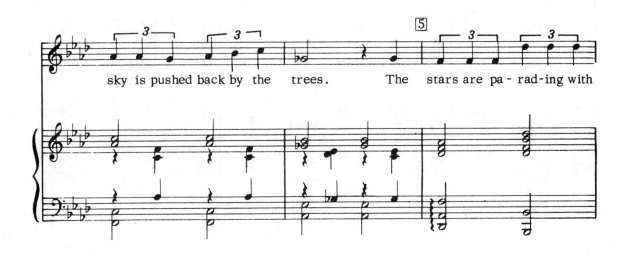

sky is pushed back by the trees. The stars are pa-rad-ing with

si-lent steps, and the moon hums a pray'r with the

226

227

30. LITTLE LAMB

(from: Songs of Innocence)
(With Piano, Four Hands Accompaniment)

Text by William Blake

Music by Gregg Smith

228

clo̲th - ing, woo̲l - y, bright! Gave thee su̲ch a̲ ten-der voice,____ You make the vales re-

joice,____ All̲ re - joice,_____ re - joice.____

dim.   [35]   p   [40]   pp

Solo I   mf   [45]

_ Lit-tle Lamb, who made thee? Dost thou know_ who made thee?_____

229

230

231

31. BROTHER WILL, BROTHER JOHN

Elizabeth Charles Welborn

John Sacco

232

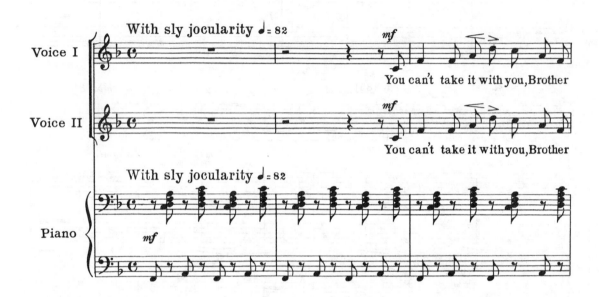

af - ter you're gone, ___ You can't take it with you, Broth - er

af - ter you're gone, ___ You can't take it with you, Broth - er

234

sly, provocative

Will, Broth - er John. Shake a leg here, ___ (clap hands)

sly, provocative

Will, Broth - er John. (clap hands) shake a leg there, ___

laugh a lit - tle, smile a lit - tle, (clap hands) Broth - er

(clap hands) (clap hands) spread a lit - tle cheer, Broth - er

32. DOWN LOW IN THE VALLEY

German Folk Song
English Version by Alice Parker

Collected by Johannes Brahms
Arranged by Ivan Trusler

238

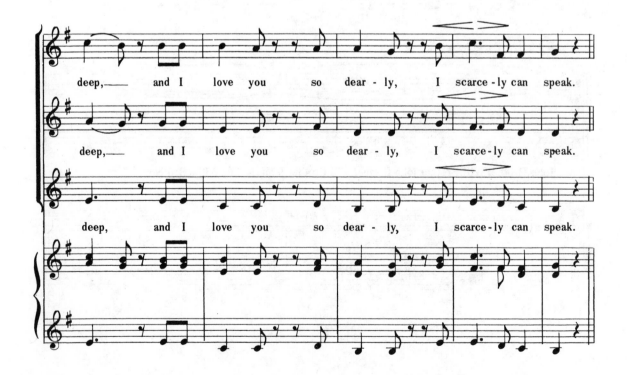

240

3. For the time that you loved me, dear, thanks give I

3. For the time that you loved me, dear, thanks give I

3. For the time that you loved me, dear, thanks give I

thee, ___ With the wish that an - o - ther love tru - er may be.

thee, ___ With the wish that an - o - ther love tru - er may be.

thee, With the wish that an - o - ther love tru - er may be.

rit.

rit.

rit.

rit.

33. THE ERIE CANAL

American Folk Song
Arranged by Robert DeCormier

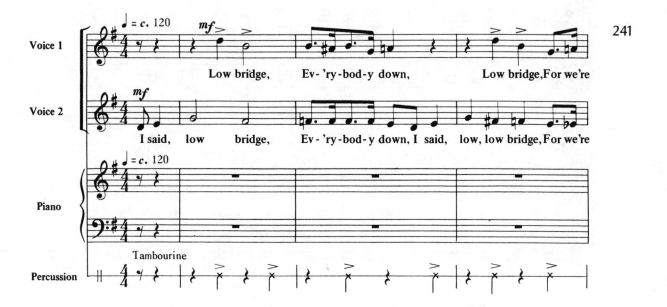

Low bridge, Ev- 'ry-bod-y down, Low bridge, For we're

I said, low bridge, Ev- 'ry-bod-y down, I said, low, low bridge, For we're

Tambourine

com-'in to a town.

com-'in to a town. I've got a mule and her

243

244

245

246

al-ways know your neigh-bor, You'll al-ways know your pal, If you've ev-er na-vi-gat-ed on the

Know your neigh-bor, know your pal, If you've ev-er na-vi-gat-ed on the

poco rit.

a tempo

Repeat 3 times, getting softer each time — fading away.

Er-ie Ca-nal.__ Low bridge, Ev-'ry-bod-y down, Low bridge, For we're

Er-ie Ca-nal.__ I said, low bridge, Ev-'ry-bod-y down, I said, low, low bridge, For we're

a tempo

1., 2.
com-'in to a town,
3.
com-'in to a town.

com-'in to a town, I said,
com-'in to a town.

pp

34. MARCH OF THE KINGS

Translated by Satis Coleman

French Folk Song
Arranged by Margaret Vance

Three great Kings I met at ear-ly morn, With all their ret-i-nue were

Three great Kings I met at ear-ly morn, With all their ret-i-nue were

Three great Kings I met at ear-ly morn, With all their

249

250

With gifts of gold brought from far a - way,

With gifts of gold brought from far a - way,

And

With gifts of gold brought from

With gifts of gold brought from

val - iant war - riors to guard the king - ly trea - sure,_ With gifts of

far a - way, __ And shields all shin - ing in their bright ar - ray.

far a - way, __ And shields all shin - ing in ar - ray.

gold, shields all shin - ing in ar - ray.

251

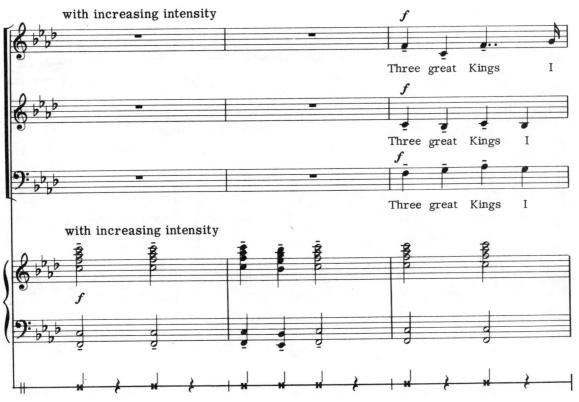

with increasing intensity

f

Three great Kings I

f

Three great Kings I

f

Three great Kings I

with increasing intensity

f

met at ear - ly morn, With all their ret-i-nue were slow - ly march - ing;

met at morn were on their way, and slow-ly_march - ing;

met at morn were on their way, and slow - ly march-ing;Those

Three great Kings I met at ear - ly morn, Were on their way to meet the

Three great Kings I met at morn, Were on their way to the

three great Kings I met at morn, Were on their way to the

35. MY LADY GREENSLEEVES
Six Madrigals on English Airs and Dances

Robert Hammond

I. The Grenadier and the Lady

Dorsetshire Folk Song

With graceful motion

254

As I was out a-walk-ing on a morn-ing__ in
With kiss-es did he ply her as he played her__ an

"O, pret-ty maid, O pret-ty, pret-ty maid,
Let me tell you what I
Let me tell you that I

May, I__ chanced to see a cou-ple, 'O, a-mak-ing of
air; "O, come close, O my__ dar-ling, and tell me you

may;__
care;__
Take__ my__ hand, make it thine,
il-lu-min-ate my
my pret-ty maid-en

hay. O,__ one was a pret-ty maid and her beau-ty shone
care." "O,__ no sir," she an-swered, "We will have one tune

day."
fair."
"O,__ no__ sir, O, no__ sir,
Tempt me not to make thee
Tempt me not__ an-y

clear, And the oth-er was a sol-dier, a bold gren-a-dier.
more, For I'll an-swer when you've played it-not a mo-ment be-fore."

dear, O,__ sir! O,__ sir, O, no__ sir, Not a gren-a-dier!"
more, O,__ sir! O,__ sir, my dear-est sir, Hold me as be-fore!"

Note: The six madrigals may be performed singly or programmed in a smaller grouping. For complete performance, the published sequence should be retained for its balance and variety and for its easy key transitions between madrigals.

II. The Wild Rover

*[By omitting the lowest voice, this "chanty" madrigal may be performed
by two-part women's chorus.]*

English traditional

III. The Turtle Dove

Dorsetshire Folk Song

256

IV. Miss Bailey's Ghost

London, 1804

V. Greensleeves

English traditional

258

Flowing

p

A - las, my love,___ you do me wrong___ To
My la - dy love,___ fare - well, a - dieu,___ To

cast me off___ dis - cour - teous - ly; And I have lov - èd
God I pray___ to pros - per thee; For I am still___ thy

you so long,___ De - light - ing in___ your com - pan - y.
lov - er true,___ Come once___ a - gain___ and love___ me.

mf

Green - sleeves was all my joy,___ Green - sleeves was my de - light;

mf

Green - sleeves was my heart of gold,___ And who but my la - dy Green-sleeves?

Green - sleeves, my heart, who but my la - dy Green-sleeves?

VI. Blowing the Candles Out

*[By omitting the lowest voice, this canonic madrigal may be performed
by two-part women's chorus.]*

17th century

With drive and spirit, but not too fast

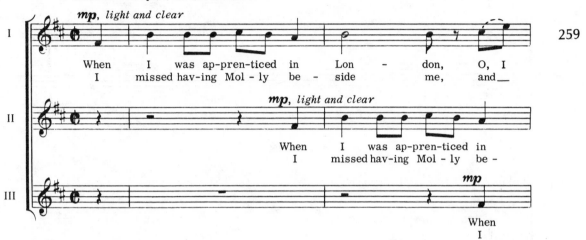

I: When I was ap-pren-ticed in Lon - don, O, I
I: I missed hav-ing Mol - ly be - side me, and

II: When I was ap-pren-ticed in
II: I missed hav-ing Mol - ly be -

III: When
III: I

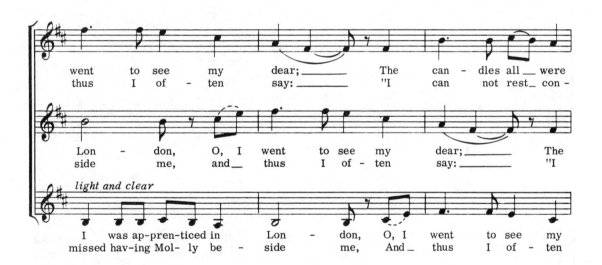

went to see my dear; The can - dles all were
thus I of - ten say: "I can not rest con -

Lon - don, O, I went to see my dear; The
side me, and thus I of - ten say: "I

I was ap-pren-ticed in Lon - don, O, I went to see my
missed hav-ing Mol- ly be - side me, And thus I of - ten

**Slightly
slower**

burn - ing, And the moon shone bright and clear. I
tent - ed While you are far a - way. The

can - dles all were burn - ing, ...and clear.
can not rest con - tent - ed... far a - way.

Mol - ly dear, I went to see Mol - ly dear.
say, I say: "I can not stay a - way.

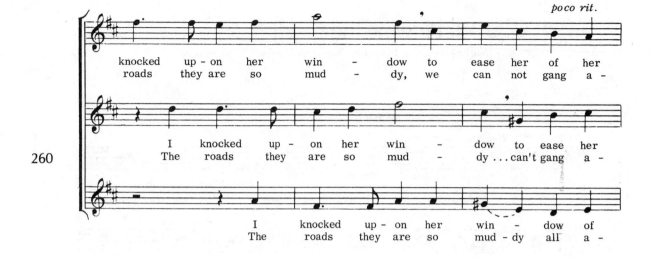

260

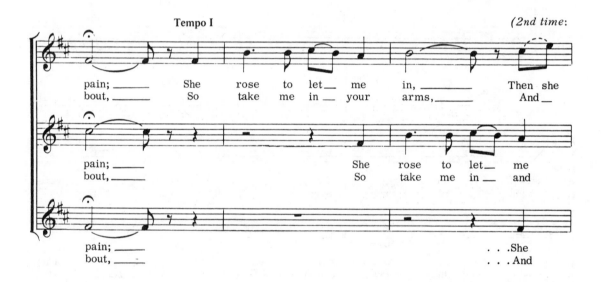

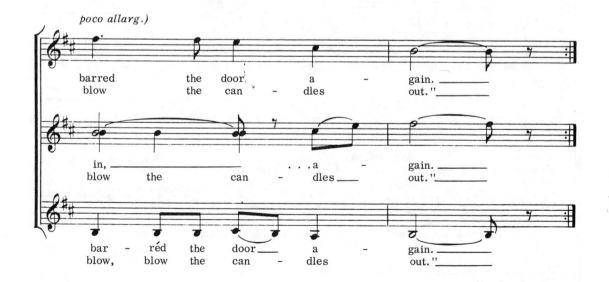

36. THE ORCHESTRA SONG

(Suitable for any combination of changed or unchanged voices)

English text by Marion Farquhar*

Traditional Austrian Song
Arranged by William Schuman

261

VIOLIN
Moderato

The fid-dles, they sing _ it and sob _ it _ and _ swing it, They sway and they play _ it, they sing _ all _ they _ say.

CLARINET

The clar-i-net, the clar-i-net says du-a, du-a, du-a, du-a-det, The clar-i-net, the clar-i-net says du-a, du-a, du-a-det.

VIOLIN

The fid-dles, they sing _ it and sob _ it _ and _

CLARINET

The clar-i-net, the clar-i-net says du-a, du-a, du-a,

swing _ it, They sway and they play _ it, they sing _ all _ they _ say.

du-a-det, The clar-i-net, the clar-i-net says du-a, du-a, du-a-det.

HORN

The horns, the horns, they shout it out, The horns, the horns, they shout it out.

*Printed by exclusive permission

VIOLIN

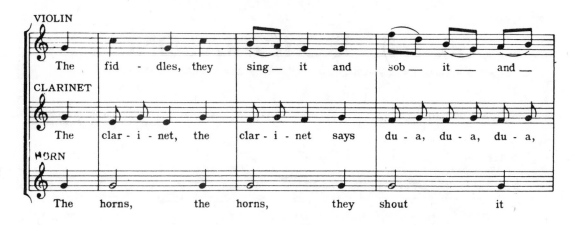

The fid - dles, they sing _ it and sob _ it _ and _

CLARINET

The clar - i - net, the clar - i - net says du - a, du - a, du - a,

HORN

The horns, the horns, they shout it

swing _ it, They sway and they play _ it, they sing _ all _ they _ say.

du - a - det, The clar - i - net, the clar - i - net says du - a, du - a, du - a - det.

out, The horns, the horns, they shout it out.

DRUM

The drum has no troub-le, just doub-le dub doub-le, Five one, one five, *bum, bum, bum, bum, bum.

VIOLIN

The fid - dles, they sing _ it and sob _ it _ and _

CLARINET

The clar - i - net, the clar - i - net says du - a, du - a, du - a,

HORN

The horns, the horns, they shout it

DRUM

The drum has no troub - le, just doub - le dub

* Pronounce to rhyme with "drum".

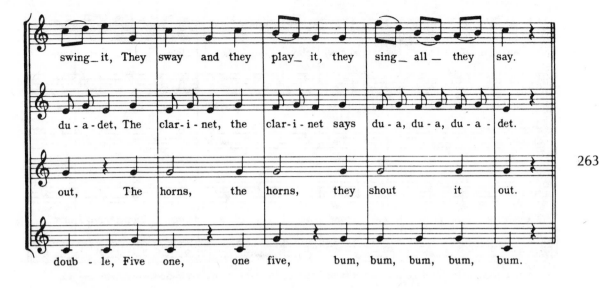

swing_ it, They sway and they play_ it, they sing_ all _ they say.

du - a - det, The clar-i-net, the clar-i-net says du - a, du - a, du - a - det.

out, The horns, the horns, they shout it out.

doub - le, Five one, one five, bum, bum, bum, bum, bum.

TRUMPET

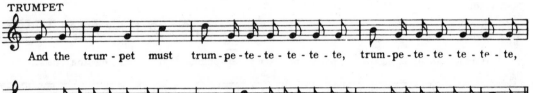

And the trum - pet must trum-pe-te-te-te, trum-pe-te-te-te,

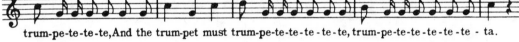

trum-pe-te-te-te, And the trum-pet must trum-pe-te-te-te-te-te, trum-pe-te-te-te-te - ta.

VIOLIN

The fid - dles, they sing_ it and sob_ it _ and _

CLARINET

The clar - i - net, the clar - i - net says du - a, du - a, du - a,

HORN

The horns, the horns, they shout it

DRUM

The drum has no troub - le, just doub - le dub

TRUMPET

And the trum - pet must trum-pe-te-te-te, trum-pe-te-te-te,

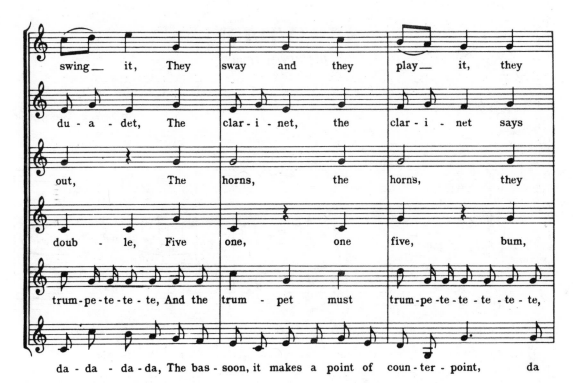

swing ___ it, They sway and they play ___ it, they
du - a - det, The clar-i-net, the clar-i-net says
out, The horns, the horns, they
doub - le, Five one, one five, bum,
trum-pe-te-te - te, And the trum - pet must trum-pe-te-te-te,
da - da - da-da, The bas-soon, it makes a point of coun-ter-point, da

265

sing ___ all ___ they ___ say. The | say. The ___ | Lo! ___
du - a, du - a, du - a - det. The | det. The ___ | Lo! ___
shout it out. The | out. The ___ | Lo! ___
bum, bum, bum, bum. The | bum. The ___ | Lo! ___
trum-pe-te-te-te-te-te - ta. And the | ta. And the | Lo! ___
da - da - da-da-da da! The bas- | da! The bas- | Lo! ___

1. May be omitted   2.   Fine

*An effective suggestion for performance is to sing these notes very long and loud, and suddenly start the last chorus _pp_

37. S'VIVON
(THE DREYDL SONG)

English text by Alicia Smith

Hanukkah Song
Arranged by Gregg Smith

266

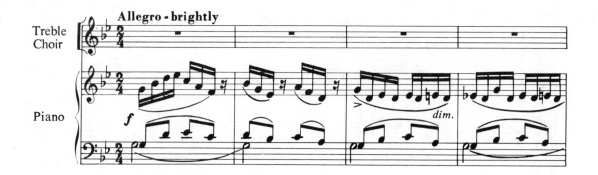

*It is preferable to sing the first verse in Hebrew and the second in English.

S' - vi - von,__ sov, sov, sov, Hag sim - ha__ hu la-- am,__
lit - tle Drey- dl, spin, spin, spin. Fes - tal lights__ now be - hold,__

nes ga - dol ha - yá__ sham,__ nes ga - dol ha - ya__ sham,__
and be joy - ful, young and old,__ And be joy - ful, young and old,__

hag sim - ha__ hu la - am!
as the mir - a - cle is told!

dim.

268

Analyses and Texts

The following outlines are intended as reference materials for the music included in this volume, rather than complete theoretical analyses.

The outlines are presented with the hope that both teachers and students may utilize them as points of departure for further study as the music is rehearsed.

270

21. HODIE CHRISTUS NATUS EST / Claudio Monteverdi (1567-1643)
(On this Day Christ is born)   (edited: Maynard Klein)

Form: motet / through-composed / sectionalized by text / phrase beginnings and
                 endings tend to overlap among the vocal parts

Tonality: modal harmony / B♭ lydian
                 final cadence uses major triad (Picardy third)

Metric Elements: ¢ meter
                 neumatic and melismatic melodic lines emphasize the flowing rhythm

Texture: polyphonic / canonic-type entrances prevail
                 three voices SSA / a cappella

Text: Latin and English

Hodie Christus natus est,	**Literal Translation**
Hodie Salvator apparuit,	Today Christ is born,
Hodie in terra canunt angeli.	Today a Savior has appeared.
Hodie in terra canunt angeli laetantur	Today the angels sing.
arcangeli.	The Archangels rejoice.
Hodie exsultant justi	Today the just rejoice,
Dicentes gloria in excelsis Deo, alleluia.	Saying glory to God on high,
	Alleluia, alleluia, alleluia.

English singing text: Maynard Klein

22. LO, HOW A ROSE E'ER BLOOMING / Michael Praetorius (1572-1621)
(arranged: David Shand)

Form: small A A B / strophic / two stanzas

Tonality: G major

Metric Elements: 3 meter / subtle syncopated rhythm
                  2

Texture: triadic
                 three voices SSA / a cappella

Text: English: Theodore Baker

23. I WILL EXTOL THEE, MY GOD / Georg Frideric Handel (1685-1759)
(arranged: Robert S. Hines)

Form:	A B C (A m. 5 / B m. 14 / C m. 20)
Tonality:	F major / A and B sections cadence on dominant C major chord
Metric Elements:	6 meter / basic rhythmic pattern of ♩♪♪ ♪♪♪ 8 prevails in the music
Texture:	chordal / the parts move in thirds in parallel motion two parts SA / keyboard accompaniment
Text:	Psalm 145: 1, 3, 9

24. SING ALOUD TO GOD / Michael Haydn (1737-1806)
(Effuderunt Sanguinem)   (edited: Reinhard G. Pauly)

Form:	sectionalized / repetition of Latin text / limited repetition of musical phrases
Tonality:	basically D major / m. 9-28 A major / m. 18-20 suggests a minor / final cadence plagal
Metric Elements:	C meter / prevalence of ♩♪♩ pattern governs tempo
Texture:	chordal / three voices SSA / keyboard accompaniment
Text:	English and Latin

Effuderunt sanguinem sanctorum
 velut aquam in circuitu Jerusalem,
Et non erat, qui sepeliret, et non erat,
 qui sepeliret.
Vindica, domine, sanguinem sanctorum
 tuorum, qui effusus, effusus est,
 super terram.

English singing text: Reinhard G. Pauly

Literal Translation
They poured out the blood
Of the innocents as water
In the vicinity of Jerusalem
And there was no one to bury them.

Avenge, Lord,
The blood of your holy ones,
Which was poured over the ground.

25. BE MERRY AND WISE / Rounds from Apollonian Harmony
(from *Apollonian Harmony*, Vol. II ca. 1790)   (edited: Jerome Gries)

Form:	ten rounds
Tonality and	Now We Are Met Let Mirth Abound / C major / 4 meter

Metric Elements: Pretty Maidens / C major / $\frac{4}{4}$ meter

Mister Speaker / C major / $\frac{6}{8}$ meter

Do, Re, Mi, So, La / G major / ¢ meter

I've Lost My Mistress, Horse and Wife / e harmonic minor / $\frac{6}{8}$ meter

Let Us Be Merry In Our Old Cloaths / D major / $\frac{6}{8}$ meter

Sir, You Are A Comical Fellow / C major / $\frac{6}{8}$ meter

Wilt Thou Lend Me Thy Mare / F major / C meter

Here's A Health / G major / $\frac{6}{8}$ meter

'Tis Hum-Drum / F major / C meter

Texture: three to five equal voices / unaccompanied

26. PRAYER / Engelbert Humperdinck (1854-1921)
   (from *Hansel and Gretel*)   (arranged: Bryceson Treharne)

Form: strophic / two stanzas with a coda

Tonality: basically C major / harmonic interest is heightened by modulatory
   chordal sequence

Metric Elements: C meter / pulse in two

Texture: homophonic
   two voices SA / piano accompaniment

Text: English
   Stanza 1 - translated from German: Constance Bache
   Stanza 2 - adapted: Willis Wagner

27. NOW'S THE TIME TO SING / Theron Kirk

Form: A B C D (following the instrumental introduction)

Tonality: B♭ major

Metric Elements: ¢   / syncopated ostinato patterns in the accompaniment support the
   brightness of mood

Texture:	homophonic
	A - presentation of the melody by Voice 1 / melody repeated in Voice 1 /
	countermelody in Voice 2
	B - melody in Voice 3 / countermelodies in Voices 1 and 2
	C - melody in Voice 2 / countermelodies in Voices 1 and 3
	D - melody in Voice 1 / countermelodies in Voices 2 and 3 / added descant
	/ melody repeated in Voice 3 / countermelodies in other voices /
	with descant / melody returned to Voice 1 / countermelodies and descant
	three treble voices / solo descant
	piano four hands accompaniment
	percussion instruments: maracas, claves, conga drum

28. FREE TO BE...YOU AND ME / Stephen Lawrence
   (arranged: Margaret Vance)

Form: A B C D Coda (B C D variations of A)
(A m. 4 / B m. 13 / C m. 33 / D m. 41 / Coda m. 60)

Tonality: Basically F major / introduction of b♮ in last twelve measures suggests key
of C major / final cadence on G major triad (dominant of C major)

Metric Elements: 4 meter / extensive use of syncopation to impart buoyant mood
4

Texture: homophonic
A - Voices 1 and 2 melody in unison
B - Voice 1 melody / Voice 2 countermelody / Voice 3 enters for last
 ten measures
C - two voices in unison
D - Voice 1 melody / Voices 2 and 3 chordal parts
two parts / optional alto / piano accompaniment

Text: Bruce Hart

29. GOOD NIGHT, LITTLE JESUS / Robert E. Page

Form: three short stanzas / A B C
(A m. 1 / B m. 9 / C m. 17)

Tonality: basically F harmonic minor

Metric Elements: C meter / pulse in slow two
frequent occurrences of triplet pattern

Texture: A - unison alto
B - melody in alto / soprano part in thirds above melody
C - melody in alto / SII part in thirds above melody / SI descant above alto
 and SII
three treble voices / piano accompaniment

Text: Robert E. Page

273

30. LITTLE LAMB / Gregg Smith

274

Form:	two stanzas with coda
Tonality:	basically F major
Metric Elements:	$\frac{3}{4}$ meter / pulse in one
Texture:	unison treble voices / piano four hands accompaniment
Text:	William Blake

31. BROTHER WILL, BROTHER JOHN / John Sacco

Form:	five short stanzas / A B C D E
Tonality:	basically F major
Metric Elements:	C meter / pulse in two / freedom of tempo indicated for expressiveness / hand claps enhance the rhythmic excitement
Texture:	homophonic two treble voices / piano accompaniment
Text:	Elizabeth Charles Welborn

32. DOWN IN THE VALLEY / German Folk Song / collected by
   Johannes Brahms (1833-1897)   (arranged: Ivan Trusler)

Form:	three stanzas / A A A′
Tonality:	G major
Metric Elements:	$\frac{3}{4}$ meter / pulse in one
Texture:	homophonic three treble voices / a cappella
Text:	Engish version: Alice Parker

33. THE ERIE CANAL / American Folk Song
  (arranged: Robert DeCormier)

Form: two stanzas with repeated refrain

Metric Elements: 4 meter / pulse in two
                     4
                     extended use of syncopation and rhythmic pattern ♩. ♪ ♩. ♪ enhance the   275
                       spirit of the music

Texture: homophonic
                     two voices SA / limited division in soprano part in interval of the third
                     piano accompaniment / tambourine and cymbal

34. MARCH OF THE KINGS / French Folk Song
  (arranged: Margaret Vance)

Form: A B C
                     (A m. 9 / B m. 19 / C m. 29)

Tonality: F harmonic minor

Metric Elements: 4 meter / recurrences of the pattern ♩. ♪ ♩. ♪
                     4
                       emphasize the vigor of the rhythmic movement

Texture: homophonic
                     A - SA in unison / T(B) enter in canon
                     B - in three parts SAT
                     C - chordal, with melody in soprano
                     three voices SAT(B) / piano accompaniment / finger cymbals

Text: English: Satis Coleman

35. MY LADY GREENSLEEVES / Robert Hammond
  (Six Madrigals on English Airs and Dances)

I The Grenadier and the Lady

Form: strophic / two stanzas

Tonality: a natural minor

Metric Elements: 3 meter / pulse in one
                     4

Texture: homophonic / two voices SA / a cappella

Text: Dorsetshire Folk Song

II The Wild Rover

Form: A A B B

Tonality: C major

Metric Elements: $\frac{3}{4}$ meter / pulse in one

Texture: homophonic
        three voices SSA / optional SS / a cappella

Text: English traditional

III The Turtle Dove

Form: strophic / two stanzas

Tonality: c natural minor

Metric Elements: $\frac{4}{4}$ meter

Texture: homophonic / two voices SA / a cappella

Text: Dorsetshire Folk Song

IV Miss Bailey's Ghost

Form: strophic / two stanzas

Tonality: B♭ major

Metric Elements: $\frac{2}{4}$ meter / the indicated accents emphasize the vitality of the
        rhythmic motion

Texture: homophonic
        two voices / a cappella

Text: London, 1804

V Greensleeves

Form: strophic / two stanzas with refrain

Tonality: basically g harmonic minor

Metric Elements: 6 meter / pulse in flowing two
8

Texture: homophonic
two voices SA / a cappella

Text: English traditional

VI Blowing the Candles Out

Form: strophic / two stanzas
each stanza: A B A'
(A m. 1 / B m. 9 / A' m. 13)

Tonality: A A' - b natural minor
B - f♯ natural minor suggested

Metric Elements: ¢   meter

Texture: A A' canonic in upper two voices / lowest voice has different melodic line
B canonic type entrances
three treble voices / lowest voice optional / a cappella

Text: Seventeenth century

36. THE ORCHESTRA SONG / Traditional Austrian Song
   (arranged: William Schuman)

Form: numerous stanzas to accommodate the text (for six orchestral instruments)

Tonality: C major

Metric Elements: 3 meter
4

Texture: I and V_7 chordal melody / texture thickens from one to six voices /
each vocal part sings a melody to represent a specific instrument / in order
of entrance: violin, clarinet, horn, drum, trumpet, bassoon / may be sung
by any combination of voices / a cappella

Text: English: Marion Farquhar

37. S'VIVON / Hanukkah Song
   (The Dreydl Song) (arranged: Gregg Smith)

Form:	A B / two stanzas
Tonality:	g harmonic minor
Metric Elements:	2 meter 4
Texture:	homophonic A - melody in unison B - Melody in soprano / harmony part in alto two voices SA / with piano accompaniment / fast ♪♪♪♪ pattern descriptive of the dreydl
Text:	Hebrew and English

278

S'vivon, sov,
Hanukkah hulag tov,
S'vivon, sov,
Hag simha hu laam,
 nes gadol haya sham,
 hag simha hu laam.

English: Alicia Smith

Music for Male Chorus

38. BOATMEN STOMP (1979)

(from: the first set of New Songs to Old Words)

The Boatmen Dance by DD. Emmett

Michael A. Gray

282

284

286

39. THE SLEIGH
(A LA RUSSE)

Ivor Tchervanow

Richard Kountz
Arranged by Wallingford Riegger

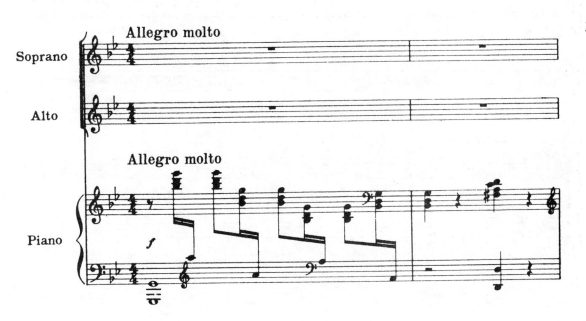

288

289

40a. SOUTH OF THE BORDER

(SAMBALELE)

(LA RASPA)

(from: Sing Out Young Voices, Vol. I)

Frederick Swanson

292   Very rhythmic but rather slowly

We got the beat from the Con - go, set it and played on the

Sing it just right, nev - er wrong - o, this is the tune of our

We got the beat from the Con - go, set it and played on the

Sing it just right, nev - er wrong - o, this is the tune of our

bon - go, song___ Oh.___ Sing it, swing it, sam - ba - le - le,

thumb on a drum all the night and the day. Dance and prance it,

sam - ba - le - le, feet to the beat that will not go a - way.

40b. PIPING TIM OF GALWAY

(from: Sing Out Young Voices, Vol. I)

Frederick Swanson

Ev - 'ry per - son in the na - tion,___
When he walks the high - way peal - ing,___

or of great or hum - ble sta - tion,___ Holds in high - est es - ti - ma - tion,
'round his head the birds go wheel - ing.___ Tim has car - ols worth the steal - ing,

297

When the wed - ding bells are ring - ing, ___

his the voice to lead the sing - ing, ___ Then in jigs the folks go swing - ing,

Pip - ing ___ Tim ___ of ___ Gal - way. He will ___ play from night till morn,

He will ___ play from night till morn,

298

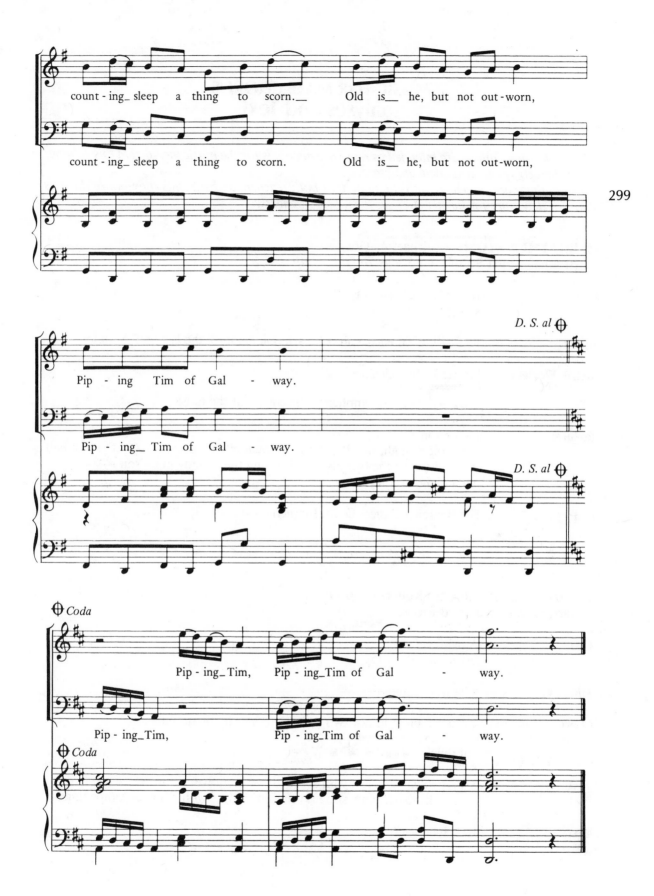

count - ing_ sleep a thing to scorn._ Old is_ he, but not out-worn,

count - ing_ sleep a thing to scorn. Old is_ he, but not out-worn,

299

D. S. al ⊕

Pip - ing Tim of Gal - way.

Pip - ing_ Tim of Gal - way.

D. S. al ⊕

⊕ *Coda*

Pip - ing_ Tim, Pip - ing_Tim of Gal - way.

Pip - ing_Tim, Pip - ing_Tim of Gal - way.

⊕ *Coda*

MUSIC FOR MALE CHORUS
Analyses and Texts

The following outlines are intended as reference materials for the music included in this volume, rather than complete theoretical analyses.

The outlines are presented with the hope that both teachers and students may utilize them as points of departure for further study as the music is rehearsed.

38. BOATMEN STOMP / Michael A. Gray
(from The First Set of *New Songs To Old Words*)

Form:	strophic / three stanzas A A A′
Tonality:	the first half of each stanza b harmonic minor / the last half A major
Metric Elements:	2 meter / the inclusion of ♩. ♩ and 4 ♫♫ patterns emphasize the energy of the music
Texture:	homophonic three voices: high, middle, low / optional pitches provided / in the first half of each stanza the two lower voices sing the melody in unison / with piano accompaniment
Text:	The Boatmen Dance: D. D. Emmett

39. THE SLEIGH / Richard Kountz (1896-1950)
(arranged: Wallingford Riegger)

Form:	A (aab) B (acd) (A. m. 3 / B m. 15)
Tonality:	g harmonic minor
Metric Elements:	4 meter / pulse in fast two / characterized by predominance 4 of quick ♩♩♩♩ ' s
Texture:	SA / two equal voices with some use of imitative entrances / when two voices have harmony soprano sings melody / with piano accompaniment
Text:	Ivor Tchervanow

40a. SOUTH OF THE BORDER / from Four Songs
(arranged: Frederick Swanson)

Form:	two dances: Sambalele and La Raspa
	Sambalele: A A B
	La Raspa: A A B
Tonality:	Sambalele - C major
	La Raspa - F major
Metric Elements:	$\frac{2}{4}$ meter / characterized by syncopated dance rhythms such as ♫♩ ♩
Texture:	two voices TB in intervals of thirds and sixths
	piano accompaniment / also bongos, castanets, claves
Text:	English

40b. PIPING TIM OF GALWAY / from Four Songs
(arranged: Frederick Swanson)

Form:	A B A Coda
Tonality:	A and Coda - D major
	B - G major
Texture:	two voices
	A - melody in bass for first half / in second half melody in tenor with harmony in bass
	B - melody in tenor for first half / in second half melody in bass with harmony in tenor
	Coda - limited division of parts in tenor
	two voices T B / with piano accompaniment

Glossary

A cappella. Sung without instrumental accompaniment.

Absolute. Absolute music. Music which is inspired by itself rather than extramusical implications such as the stories or legends of "program" music.

Accelerando, accel. Gradually faster.

Accent. ≻ placed above a note to indicate stress or emphasis.

Accidental. A sharp, flat, or natural not included in the given key.

Adagio. Slow; slower than **andante**, faster than **largo**.

Ad libitum, ad lib. A term which permits the performer to vary the tempo and/or to include or omit a vocal or instrumental part. Synonymous with **a piacere**.

A due. Return to unison after **divisi**.

Agilmente. Lively.

Agitato. Agitated; with excitement.

Al. To; used with other words, e.g. **al Fine** (to the end).

Aleatory, or **aleatoric music**. Chance music in which the performers are free to perform their own material and/or their own manner of presentation.

Alla breve. ₵ Cut time; meter in which there are two beats in each measure and a half note receives one beat.

Allargando, allarg. Slowing of tempo, usually with increasing volume; most frequently occurs toward the end of a piece.

Allegretto. Slower than **allegro**.

Allegro. Quick tempo; cheerful.

Alto, contralto. The lowest female voice.

Ancora. Repeat.

Andante. Moderate tempo.

Andantino. Slightly faster than **andante**.

A niente. To nothing, e.g. to **ppp**.

Animato. Animated; lively.

Anthem. English choral composition with sacred words. Comparable to the **motet**.

Antiphon. A term for various types of Gregorian chant. Also applied to some chants of the Mass: Introit, Offertory, and Communion.

Antiphonal. Style of singing by alternating choirs.

A piacere. Freedom in performance. Synonymous with **ad libitum**.

Appassionato. Impassioned.

Appoggiatura. A nonharmonic tone, usually a half or whole step above the harmonic tone, which is performed on the beat and then resolved.

Aria. A song for one or two solo voices, found in cantatas, oratorios, and operas.

Arpeggio. A term used to describe the pitches of a chord as they are sung or played one after the other, rather than simultaneously.

Articulation. The movement of the articulating organs, especially the lips, to form intelligible sounds.

A tempo. Return to the previous tempo.

Atonality. Lacking a tonal center.

Augmentation. Compositional technique in which a melodic line is repeated in longer note values. The opposite of **diminution**.

Augmented. The term for a major or perfect **interval** which has been enlarged by one half-step, e.g. c-g ♯, (an augmented fifth,) or c-d ♯, (an augmented second). Also used for a triad with an augmented fifth, e.g. the augmented tonic triad in C major, C+, c-e-g ♯.

Ayre. Air. A tune or melody. A song for one voice or for several voices.

Ballad. A narrative song.

Ballade. In the medieval period a form of **trouvère** music and poetry. In later time, German poetry set as a through-composed song.

Ballata. A principal form of Italian poetry and music in the 14th century.

Ballett, balletto. Renaissance part song which used fa-la refrain.

Baritone. The male voice between bass and tenor.

Bar line. The vertical line placed on the staff to divide the music into measures.

Baroque. The period 1600-1750.

Bass. The lowest male voice. Also the other name for the F clef.

Basso continuo. Continuo. Thorough-bass. The Baroque practice in which the bass part is played by a viola da gamba (cello) or bassoon while a keyboard instrument performed the bass line and the indicated chords.

Battuto. Beat, bar, or measure. **A due** or **a tre battuta**, the musical rhythm in groups of two or three respectively.

Bel canto. 18th century vocal technique which emphasized beautiful sound and virtuosic performance.

Ben. Well. Used with other words, e.g. **ben marcato**, well accented, emphasized.

Binary form. The term for describing a composition of two sections. AB, each of which may be repeated.

Bitonality. The occurrence of two different tonalities at the same time.

Cadence. A chordal or melodic progression which occurs at the close of a phrase, section, or composition, giving a feeling of repose; a temporary or permanent ending. The most frequently used cadences are **perfect, plagal,** and **deceptive**.

Calmo, calmato. Calm.

Cambiata. A term meaning change, applied to a boy's changing voice.

Canon. The strictest form of imitation, in which two or more parts have the same **melody** but start at different points.

Canonic. A term used to describe a polyphonic style of music in which all the parts have the same melody but which start at different times.

Cantabile. In singing style.

Cantata. Baroque sacred or secular choral composition containing solos, duets, and choruses, with orchestral or keyboard accompaniment.

Canticle. A song, chant, or hymn with a Biblical text, used in church liturgy.

Cantor. Solo singer in both Catholic and Jewish services. The term also used for the director of music in the early Protestant church.

Cantus firmus. A pre-existing tune to which other voices, or parts, are added to make a polyphonic composition.

Canzonette. Smaller form of **canzona**. A 16th-century short dance-like vocal composition.

Carol. The term was derived from a medieval French word, *carole*, a circle dance. In England it was first associated with pagan songs celebrating the winter solstice. It then developed into a song of praise and celebration, usually for Christmas.

Catch. 17th-18th-century rounds of comical character.

Chance music. Aleatoric music.

Chanson. The French term for song. In the 16th century it was imitative in style. In the 17th and 18th centuries it was usually a popular, short **strophic** song.

Chant, plainsong. The general term for liturgical music with these characteristics: **monophonic**, in free rhythm, unaccompanied, of limited vocal range.

304

Chantey, shanty. Working songs of English and American sailors.

Chorale. Hymn-like song, characterized by blocked chords.

Chord. A combination of three or more tones sounded simultaneously.

Chorister. A singer in a choir. In early usage it referred to a boy singer in an English choir.

Chromatic. Ascending or descending by half steps.

Classicism. In music, the term usually denotes the period 1770-1825.

Clef. A symbol placed at the beginning of the **staff** to indicate the **pitch** of the notes on the staff. The most commonly used clefs in choral music are the G, or treble, clef 𝄞 and the F, or bass clef 𝄢 . On the keyboard, all the notes above middle C are said to be in the G clef; all the notes below middle C in the F clef.

Coda. Closing section of a composition. An added ending.

Con. With.

Con brio. With spirit; vigorously.

Con calore. With warmth.

Concertato. A term used to describe a 17th-century style or texture which emphasized contrast between voices and instruments or between solo voices and groups of voices.

Con intensità. With intensity.

Conjunct. Pitches on successive degrees of the scale; opposite of **disjunct.**

Con moto. With motion.

Consonance. Intervallic relationships which produce sounds of repose. Frequently associated with octave, third and sixth intervals; however, fourths and fifths may be sounds of consonance, as in both early and 20th-century music.

Consort. A 17th-century term for instrumental chamber ensembles and for the compositions written for these ensembles.

Con spirito. With spirit.

Contrapuntal. Descriptive of **counterpoint;** the texture in which two or more voices move independently.

Countermelody. A vocal part which contrasts with the principal **melody.**

Counterpoint. The technique of combining single melodic lines or parts of equal importance.

Crescendo. < Gradually louder.

Da capo, D. C. Return to the beginning.

Dal segno, D. S. Repeat from the sign 𝄋 . Frequently followed by **al Fine.**

Deceptive cadence. Chordal progression dominant (V) to a chord other than the expected tonic.

Decrescendo. > Gradually softer. Synonymous with **diminuendo.**

Degree. One of the eight consecutive tones in a major or minor scale.

Delicato. Delicately.

Descant. A countermelody, usually above the principal melody, to be sung by a few voices.

Diaphragm. The muscular area which separates the chest cavity and the abdomen. An important muscle in the inhalation/exhalation cycle.

Diminished. The term for an **interval** which has been decreased from the major by two half steps and from the perfect by one half step, e.g. c-a♭♭, diminished sixth, or c-g♭, a diminished fifth. Also used for a **triad** which has a minor third and a diminished fifth, e.g. c♭, c-e♭, g♭

Diminuendo, dim. Gradually softer. Synonymous with **decrescendo.**

Diminution. The shortening of note values; the opposite of **augmentation.**

Diphthong. Two successive vowels on one syllable.

Disjunct. The term used to describe **intervals** larger than a second; the opposite of **conjunct.**

Dissonance. Sounds of unrest, e.g. **intervals** of seconds and sevenths; the opposite of **consonance.**

Divisi, div. An indication of divided vocal parts, e.g. SI and SII.

Do. The first degree of the major scale.

Dolce. Sweetly.

Dolcissimo. Very sweetly.

Doloroso. Sadly; mournfully.

Dominant. The fifth degree of the major or minor scale. Also, the term for the **triad** built on the fifth degree, labelled V in harmonic analysis.

Dorian. The first **Medieval church** mode. Its **pitches** are arranged in this pattern:

whole half whole whole whole half whole
step step step step step step step

Double bar. Two vertical lines placed on the **staff** to indicate the end of a section or a composition. Also, used with two dots to enclose repeated sections.

Double flat. ♭♭ A symbol for lowering pitch one step.

Double sharp. × A symbol for raising pitch one step.

Duplet. ♩♩ A group of two notes performed in the time of three of the same kind.

Duplum. In **organa** of the 12th century the part above the tenor; in the 13th century **motet** the **duplum** was called the **motetus.**

Dynamics. Varying degrees of loud and soft.

E. Italian word meaning "and."

Enharmonic. A term used to describe notes of the same pitch which have different names, e.g. c♯ and d♭, f♯ and g♭.

Enunciation. The manner of speaking and singing words as it pertains to distinct vowels and consonants.

Espressivo. Expressively.

Esuberante. Exuberant.

Fa. In **solmization**, the fourth degree of the major scale.

Falsetto. The voice of the male singer as it reproduces pitches which lie beyond its normal range.

Fasola. A system of **solmization** used in 17th- and 18th-century England and America. Fa, so, and la were given to both c-d-e and f-g-a, with mi used for the seventh degree.

Fermata. Hold; pause.

Festivo. Festive; merry.

Fifth. The fifth degree of the diatonic scale. Also, the interval formed by a given tone and the fifth tone above or below it, e.g. c up to g, c down to f. Intervals of the fifth may be **perfect** (corresponding to major), **diminished,** or **augmented.**

Fine. The end.

First ending. One or more **measures** which occur at the end of the stanza or stanzas. It is usually indicated :

Fixed do. The system of **solmization** in which c is always **do**.

Flat. ♭ A symbol which lowers the pitch of a note one-half step.

Form. The design or structure of a musical composition.

Forte. *f* Loud.

Fortissimo. *ff* Very loud.

Fourth. The fourth degree of the diatonic scale. Also, the interval formed by a given tone and the fourth tone above or below it, e.g. c up to f; c down to g. Intervals of the fourth may be **perfect, diminished,** or **augmented.**

Frottola. A type of Italian poetry and music of the Renaissance. In chordal style, of three or four parts, the music is arranged in several short repeated sections. Today, the term **frottola** may include song types such as **canzona** and **ode.**

Fugal. Descriptive term for contrapuntal style.

Fz. Forzando or forzato. Synonomous with **sforzando** (*sf or sfz*).

Giocoso. Playful.

Giubilante. Exultant, jubilant.

Glee. 18th century unaccompanied song, in three or more parts, for men's voices.

Glissando. Gliss. The rapid **scale** achieved by sliding the nail of the thumb or third finger over the white keys of the piano. Glissando is commonly used in playing the harp. For bowed instruments glissando indicates a flowing, unaccented playing of a passage.

Glottis. The opening between the vocal cords.

Grandioso. Grandiose, majestic.

Grand staff, Great staff. The G and F clef staves together make the grand (great) staff.

Grave. Slow, solemn.

Grazia. Grace. Con grazia, with grace.

Grazioso. Graceful.

Gregorian chant. The liturgical chant of the Roman Catholic Church, named for Pope Gregory I.

Half step. The interval from one pitch to the immediately adjacent pitch, ascending or descending, e.g. c-c♯ ; e-e♭ ; b-c. The smallest interval on the keyboard.

Harmony. The sounding of two or more tones simultaneously; the vertical aspect of music.

Hemiola. The term applied to time values in the ration of 3:2, e.g. three half notes in place of two dotted half notes.

Homophony. Homophonic. Musical **texture** which is characterized by chordal support of a melodic line.

Imitation. The recurrence of a melodic line in different voices, or parts, e.g. **round, canon.**

Impressionism. A musical movement of the late 19th and early 20th centuries. Inspired by the French impressionist painters, the movement had its impetus in the music of Debussy and Ravel.

Interval. The difference in pitch between two tones.

Inversion. As applied to music the term may be used in both melody and harmony. **Melodic inversion:** an exchange of ascending and descending movement, e.g. c up to f in descending becomes c down to g. **Harmonic inversion:** the position of the chord is changed from root position (root on the lowest pitch) to first inversion, with the third, or second inversion, with the fifth in the lowest voice. An example: root position c-e-g; first inversion e-g-c; second inversion g-c-e.

Ironico. Ironical.

Key signature. The sharps or flats placed at the beginning of the staff to denote the scale upon which the music is based.

La. In **solmization**, the sixth degree of the major scale. Also, the first degree of the relative minor scale, e.g. a is the sixth degree, or la, in the C major scale and the first degree of the a-minor scale.

Lamento. Mournful, sad.

Langsam. Slow.

Larghetto. Slower than **largo**.

Largo. Very slow.

Larynx. The structure of muscle and cartilage at the upper end of the trachea, or windpipe, which contains the vocal cords.

Leading tone. The seventh degree of the major scale, so called because of its strong tendency to resolve upward to the **tonic**.

Ledger lines. Short lines placed above and below the staff for pitches beyond the range of the staff.

Legato. Smooth, connected.

Leggiero. Light; graceful.

Lento. Slow; slightly faster than **largo**, slower than **adagio**.

Liberamento. Freely.

Lied, plural **lieder**. German art song, especially prominent in 19th-century music literature. Characterized by the union of poetry and music.

Linear. Melodic; horizontal lines.

Liturgical. Pertaining to prescribed forms of worship or ritual in various Christian church services. The development of Western music received its impetus from music written for the liturgy of the early Catholic church.

Lydian. The third **medieval church mode.** Its **pitches** are arranged in this intervallic pattern:
whole whole whole half whole whole half
step step step step step step step

Ma. But. Used with other words, e.g. **lento ma non troppo**, slow but not too slowly.

Madrigal. A vocal form, originating in Italy in the 14th century which reached its highest point of development in England and Italy in the 16th and 17th centuries. English **madrigals** sometimes had other names such as **sonets, canzonets, ayres.**

Maestoso. Majestically.

Major. The designation for certain intervals and scales. A key based on a major scale is called a major key. The pattern for the major scale is:
whole whole half whole whole whole half
step step step step step step step

Marcato. Emphasized, heavily accented.

Mass. A musical setting of the most solemn service in the Roman Catholic Church.

Measure. A group of beats containing a primary accent and one or more secondary accents, indicated by the placement of bar lines on the staff.

Mediant. The third degree of the major or minor scale. The triad build on this degree is labeled iii in the major scale, III in the natural minor scale, and III$^+$ in the harmonic minor scale.

Medieval. The period prior to the Renaissance, c. 500-1450, marking the music of the early Christian church.

Melisma. Melismatic. A melodic line, as originating in Gregorian chant, in which one syllable is sung on several pitches; in contrast to **neumatic** and **syllabic.**

Melodic minor. One of the three **minor modes** or **scales** (See Minor-Natural and Harmonic). Ascending, the **melodic minor scale** is the same as the **major scale** with the exception of the flatted third **degree**. Descending, the sixth and seventh **degrees**, in addition to the third **degree** are flatted. Example:

C melodic minor scale

Melody. In general, a succession of musical tones. It represents the linear or horizontal aspect of music.

Meno. Less.

Meno mosso. Less motion.

Meter. The structure of notes in a regular pattern of accented and unaccented beats within a measure, indicated at the beginning of a composition by a meter signature.

Meter signature. The numbers placed at the beginning of a composition to indicate the meter of the music, e.g. $\frac{3}{4}$, $\frac{6}{8}$, $\frac{2}{2}$. The upper number indicates the beats in a measure; the lower number tells what kind of a note will receive one beat.

Metronome. Invented by Maelzel in 1816, the instrument is used to indicate the exact tempo of a composition. An indication such as M.M. 60 indicates that the pendulum, with a weight at the bottom, makes 60 beats per minute. A slider is moved up and down the pendulum to decrease and increase the tempo. M.M. ♩ = 80 means that the time value of a quarter note is the equivalent of one pendulum beat when the slider is set at 80.

Mezzo forte. *mf* Medium loud.

Mezzo piano. *mp* Medium soft.

Mezzo voce. With half voice; reduced volume of tone.

Mi. In **solmization**, the third degree of the major scale.

Minor. The designation for certain intervals and scales. A key based on a minor scale is called a minor key. The three types of minor scales include natural, harmonic, and melodic, which is used infrequently in choral music. The patterns for natural and harmonic scales are:

natural:	whole step	half step	whole step	whole step	half step	whole step	whole step
harmonic:	whole step	half step	whole step	whole step	whole step	1½ steps	half step

Mixed voices. A combination of male and female voices.

Mode. Any scalewise arrangement of pitches; more generally, the term refers to the patterns upon which medieval music was structured, the patterns which preceded the development of major and minor scales and tonality.

Moderato. Moderate speed.

Modulation. The process of changing from one key to another within a composition.

Molto. Very. Used with other terms, e.g. **molto allegro**.

Monophony. Monophonic. The texture of music in which there is a single unaccompanied melodic line.

Morendo. Gradually decreasing in volume; dying away.

Mosso. Rapid. Meno mosso, less rapid. Più mosso, more rapid.

Motet. An important medieval and Renaissance **polyphonic** song. After many changes in its development, it is generally considered as an unaccompanied sacred choral composition, frequently in contrapuntal style.

Motive. A short melodic or rhythmic pattern.

Moto. Motion. Con moto, with motion.

Movable Do. The system of solmization in which **do** changes to accommodate the key, e.g. in the key of C major, **do** is c; in E♭ major **do** is e♭ . In the key of a minor **do** is c (relative major); in the key of c minor **do** is e♭ (relative major).

Natural. ♮ A musical symbol which cancels a previous sharp or flat.

Neumatic. One style of chant in which two to four pitches occur on one syllable; in contrast to **melismatic** and **syllabic**.

Nonharmonic tones. A designation for tones outside the harmonic structure of the chord. Two frequently used examples are the **passing tone** and the **appoggiatura**.

Non troppo. Not too much. Used with other terms, e.g. **non troppo allegro**, not too fast.

Notation. A term for a system of expressing musical sounds through the use of written characters, called **notes**.

Note. The symbol which, when placed on a staff with a particular clef sign, indicates pitch.

Nuance. Sublte variations in tempo, phrasing, dynamics, etc., to enhance a musical performance.

Octave. The eighth tone above a given pitch, with twice as many vibrations per second, or below a given pitch, with half as many vibrations.

Opera. A drama in which lines are sung, rather than spoken, by soloists and choruses accompanied by an orchestra.

Operetta. Light opera which includes sung and spoken dialogue, solo voices, chorus, orchestra, and dance.

Opus. Op. The term, meaning work, is used by composers to show the chronological order of their works, e.g. Op. 1, Op. 2.

Oratorio. An extended work, generally sacred in character, frequently with a Biblical text, performed without dramatic action, for solo voices, chorus, and orchestra.

Ordinary. The part of the Mass which remains the same for different days. Its sections include Kyrie, Gloria, Credo, Sanctus, and Agnus Dei.

Organum. The first polyphonic writing in Western music, begun in the 9th century and based on **plainsong** melodies. The first **organa** were for two voices moving in parallel fourths and fifths. As music developed, more voice parts were added.

Ornamentation. Note or notes added to the original melodic line for embellishment and added interest.

Ostinato. A repeated melodic or rhythmic pattern, frequently appearing in the bass line.

Overtones. The almost inaudible higher tones which occur with the fundamental tone. They are the result of the vibration of small sections of a string (instrument) or a column of air. Other general terms for **overtones** are **partials** and **harmonics**.

Palate. The roof of the mouth. The hard palate is the forward part; the soft palate, or **velum**, the back part.

Parallel motion. The movement of two or more voice parts in the same direction, at the same interval from each other.

Parlando. A combination of speech and song.

Passing tones. Unaccented notes which move conjunctly between two chords to which they do not belong harmonically.

Passion. A musical setting of the Biblical text of the Passion. Like **oratorio**, it may include solo voices, chorus, and orchestra or organ.

Patschen. Thigh slap.

Pensieroso. Contemplative, thoughtful.

Perfect. A term used to label fourth, fifth, and octave intervals. It corresponds to the major, as given to seconds, thirds, sixths, and sevenths.

Perfect cadence. The chordal progression of dominant to tonic, in a major key V-I, in minor V-i.

Pesante. Heavy.

Phrase. A relatively short portion of a melodic line which expresses a musical idea, comparable to a line or sentence in poetry.

Piano. *p* Soft.

Pianissimo. *pp* Very soft.

Picardy third. The term for the raising of the third, making a major triad, in the final chord of a composition which is in a minor key. The practice originated in c. 1500 and extended through the Baroque period.

Pitch. The highness or lowness of a tone, as determined by the number of vibrations in the sound.

Più. More. Used with other terms, e.g. **più mosso**, more motion.

Plagal cadence. Sometimes called the **"amen" cadence.** The chordal progression of subdominant to tonic, in a major key IV-I, in minor iv-i.

Plainsong. Chant. A general term for the monophonic, unmetered melody of the liturgy of the early Christian church.

Poco. Little. Used with other terms, e.g. **poco accel.**, also, **poco a poco**, little by little.

Poco ced., Cedere. A little slower.

Poco più mosso. A little more motion.

Poi. Then or afterwards, e.g. **poi No. 3**, then No. 3.

Polyphony. Polyphonic. Music in which two or more parts or voices move independently.

Polyrhythm. The simultaneous occurrence of two or more contrasting rhythms.

Polytonality. The occurrence of several different tonalities at the same time.

Presto. Very quick.

Primo. First.

Proper. The part of the Mass in which the texts vary to fit the particular service.

Quartal harmony. A term which has come into use in the 20th century to describe music based on chords arranged in intervals of fourths.

Quasi. Almost. Used with other terms, e.g. **quasi madrigal**, almost or as if a **madrigal**.

Rallentando, rall. Gradually slower. Synonymous with **ritardando**.

Range. The gamut of pitches, from low to high, which a singer may perform.

Rapide. Rapidly.

Re. In **solmization**, the second degree of the major scale.

Recitative. Declamatory style of singing. It is characterized by free rhythm and clarity of text.

Refrain. A short section of repeated material which occurs at the end of each stanza.

Register. A term used to denote the characteristics of the different ranges of the human voice, e.g. "chest register," or "head register."

Relative major and minor scales. Major and minor scales which have the same key signature.

Renaissance. The period c. 1450-1600.

Repeat. The reptition of a section or a composition as indicated by particular signs.
Repeat of a section: ‖: :‖
Repeat from the beginning: :‖
Also **D.C.**, repeat from the beginning and **D.S.**, repeat from the sign.

Resonance. Reinforcement and intensification of sound by vibrations.

Responsorial singing. The alternation of phrases by a soloist and a chorus.

Rest. A symbol used to denote silence.

Retrograde. The term for the performance of a melody in reverse, or backward. Synonymous with **crab motion**.

Rhythm. The term which denotes the organization of sound in time; the temporal quality of sound.

Risoluto. Resolute.

Ritardando, rit. Gradually slower. Synonymous with **rallentando**.

Ritenuto. Immediate reduction in tempo.

Ritmico. Rhythmically.

Romanticism. The period c. 1825-1900.

Root. The note upon which a triad or chord is built.

Root position. The arrangement of a chord in which the root is in the lowest voice.

Round. Like the **canon**, a song in which two or more parts having the same **melody**, starting at different points. The parts may be repeated as desired.

Rubato. The term used to denote flexibility of tempo to assist in achieving expressiveness.

Ruhig. Quiet.

Rustico. Pastoral.

Scale. A succession of tones. The scale is generally used in Western music is the **diatonic** scale, consisting of whole and half steps in a specific order.

Schola Cantorum. Literally, a school of singers. The term originally described a 4th-century papal choir and singing school.

Secco. Dry. The term was used in the 18th-century to describe the unexpressive nature of the recitative.

Second. The second degree of the diatonic scale. Also, the interval formed by a given tone and the next tone above or below it, e.g. c up to d, or c down to b. Intervals of the second may be major, diminished, or augmented.

Section. A division of a musical composition.

Sehr leise beginnend. Very soft in the beginning.

Semitone. A half step. The smallest interval on the keyboard.

Sempre. Always. Used with other terms, e.g. **sempre staccato**.

Semplice. Simple.

Senza. Without. Used with other terms, e.g. **senza crescendo**.

Sequence. The repetition of a melodic pattern on a higher or lower pitch level.

Seventh. The seventh degree of the diatonic scale. Also, the interval formed by a given tone and the seventh tone above or below it, e.g. c up to b, or c down to d. Intervals of the seventh may be major, minor, diminished, or augmented.

Seventh chord. When a seventh (above the root) is added to a triad (root, third, fifth), the result is a seventh chord, e.g. the dominant triad in the key of C major, g-b-d, with the added seventh becomes g-b-d-f and is labelled V^7.

Sforzando. Sfz. Sf. Sudden strong accent on a note or chord.

Sharp. ♯ A symbol which raises the pitch of a note one-half step.

Shifting meter. The changing of meter within a composition. Synonymous with **changing meter**.

Simile. An indication to continue in the same manner.

Six-four chord. The second inversion of a triad, made by placing the fifth of the chord in the lowest voice, e.g. C_4^6 is g-c-e.

Sixth. The sixth degree of the diatonic scale. Also, the interval formed by a given tone and the sixth tone above or below it, e.g. c up to a, or c down to e. Intervals of the sixth may be major, minor, diminished, or augmented.

Sixth chord. The first inversion of a triad, made by placing the third of the chord in the lowest voice, e.g. C_6 is e-g-c.

Slur. A curved line placed above or below two or more notes of different pitch to indicate that they are to be performed in **legato** style.

Sol. In **solmization**, the fifth degree of the major scale.

Sognando. Dreamily.

Solfège. A vocal exercise sung on vowels or the syllables of **solmization**. Also used as a term to describe the study of the rudiments of music.

Solmization. The term for the use of syllables for the degrees of the major scale: do, re, mi, fa, sol, la ti, do. The minor scale (natural) is la, ti, do, re, mi, fa, sol, la.

Soprano. The highest female voice. Types include mezzo, lyric, dramatic, and coloratura.

Sostenuto. Sustaining of tone or slackening of tempo.

Sotto voce. Under the voice, i.e. in a quiet, subdued voice.

Sprechstimme. A 20th-century term to describe speech song.

Staccato. Detached sounds, indicated by a dot over or under a note. The opposite of **legato**.

Staff. The most frequently used staff has five horizontal lines, with four spaces, upon which the notes and other musical symbols are placed.

Strophic. A term used to describe a song in which all the stanzas of the text are sung to the same music. The opposite of **through-composed**.

Subdominant. The fourth degree of the major or minor scale. Also, the name of the triad built on the fourth degree of the scale, indicated by IV in a major key and by iv in a minor key.

Subito. Suddenly.

Submediant. The sixth degree of the major or minor scale. Also, the name of the triad built on the sixth degree of the scale, indicated by VI in a major key and by vi in a minor key.

Supertonic. The second degree of the major or minor scale. Also, the name of the triad built on the second degree of the scale, indicated by II in a major scale and ii° in a minor scale.

Suspension. The use of a **nonharmonic** tone to delay the resolution of a chord, frequently as it occurs in a **cadence**.

Susurrando. Whispering.

Syncopation. Accent on an unexpected beat.

Tactus. The 15th- and 16th-century term for beat.

Tempo. The rate of speed in a musical work.

Tempo primo. Return to the original tempo.

Teneramente. Tenderly.

Tenor. The highest male voice.

Tenuto, ten. Hold or sustain a note longer than the indicated value, usually not as long a duration as the **fermata**.

Ternary form. Three-part form in which the middle section is different from the other sections. Indicated by ABA.

Terraced dynamics. The Baroque style of using sudden changes in dynamic levels, as opposed to gradual increase and decrease in volume.

Tertian harmony. A term used to describe music based on chords arranged in intervals of thirds.

Tessitura. The general pitch range of a vocal part.

Text painting. The music as written by the composer to enhance the text. Examples: ascending pitches for words such as *exultavit, alleluia*; lower pitches and minor keys for words such as *weeping, dolor*.

Texture. The term used to describe the way in which melodic lines are combined, either with or without accompaniment. Types include **monophonic, homophonic,** and **polyphonic,** or **contrapuntal.**

Third. The third degree of the diatonic scale. Also, the interval formed by a given tone and the third tone above or below it, e.g. c up to e, or c down to a. Intervals of the third may be major, minor, diminished, or augmented.

Through-composed. A term used to describe a song in which the music for each stanza is different. The opposite of **strophic.**

Ti. In **solmization,** the seventh degree of the major scale. Also called the **leading tone.**

Tie. A curved line over or below two or more notes of the same pitch. The first pitch is sung or played and held for the duration of the notes affected by the **tie.**

Timbre. The characteristic quality of a voice or instrument.

Time signature. Synonymous with **meter signature.**

Tonality. The term used to describe the organization of the melodic and harmonic elements to give a feeling of a key center or a tonic pitch.

Tone clusters. The simultaneous sounding of two or more adjacent tones.

Tonic. The first note of a key. Also, the name of the chord built on the first degree of the scale, indicated by I in a major key or i in a minor key.

Tranquillo. Tranquilly; quietly.

Transposition. The process of changing the key of a composition.

Tre. Three. Used with other terms, e.g. **a tre voci,** in three parts.

Triad. A chord of three tones arranged in thirds, e.g. the C-major triad c-e-g, root-third-fifth.

Trill. tr. A musical **ornament** performed by the rapid alternation of a given note with a **major** or **minor** second above.

Triphthong. The occurrence of three successive vowels on one syllable.

Triple meter. Meter based on three beats, or a multiple of three, in a measure.

Triplet. ♩ ♩ ♩ A group of three notes performed in the time of two of the same kind.

Troppo. Too much. Used with other terms, e.g. **allegro non troppo,** not too fast.

Turn. ∞ A musical ornament characterized by the rapid performance of a given **note,** the **major** or **minor** second above and below, and a return to the given **note.**

Tutti. All. A direction for the entire ensemble to sing or play simultaneously.

Twelve-tone technique. A system of composition which uses the twelve tones of the **chromatic scale** in an arbitrary arrangement called a tone row or series. The row may be used in its original **form,** its **inversion,** in **retrograde,** and in the **inversion** of the **retrograde.** The system was devised by Arnold Schoenberg in the early 20th century.

Unison. Singing or playing the same notes by all singers or players, either at exactly the same pitch or in a different octave.

Un peu. A little. Used with other words, e.g. **un peu piano.**

Upbeat. One or more notes occurring before the first bar line, as necessitated by the text for the purpose of desirable accent, e.g. 3/4 ♩ | ♩. ♪ ♩ |

The night -in- gale

Variation. The manipulation of a theme by the use of melodic, rhythmic, and harmonic changes.

Verse. A line of poetry. Frequently used to denote a stanza of a poem.

Villanelle. Villanesca. A rustic song. A 16th-century Italian song of less refinement than the **madrigal** of the period.

Vivace. Lively.

Vivo. Lively.

Voce. Voice.

314   **Whole step**. The interval made by two half steps.

Wholetone scale. A scale made up entirely of whole tones.

APPENDICES

APPENDIX A

The Development of Music Notation

Music, as it is notated today, is a legacy which dates back to the civilization of the ancient Greeks. "Music" is a Greek word which means "inspired by the Muses." The Greeks developed a tonal system which has become the basis of most of the music of the Western world.

The system of representing the sounds of the songs in this book by graphic symbols took centuries to develop. Both the ancient Greeks and the Romans used letters of their alphabets to represent sounds. The Greeks used other signs to represent time patterns.

The singers of the early Christian church gradually developed melodies from the chanted prayers and psalms of their worship services. Monks trained choirs of men and boys to sing these chants by rote. By the eighth century, the body of chants had grown so large it was difficult for the choirs to remember all of them.

Something more specific than the gestures used by the monks to indicate higher and lower pitches was needed, so the monks experimented with the use of neumes. These curved lines placed above each word indicated where the voices should rise and where they should fall. The first neumes indicated only the general contour of a melody, simply aiding the singer in remembering the chants he had been taught by repetition. As more shapes were added, the singer was able to approximate pitches indicated by the shaped notes.

Early notes were square shaped because of the use of quill pens. The music was written by monks by hand and was often beautifully illustrated. These manuscripts took many months to complete.

Just as the Greeks and Romans had done, the monks named pitches after letters of the alphabet. The eleventh-century monk Guido of Arezzo taught his pupils to relate syllables to tones. Taking the syllables ut, re, mi, fa, sol, la from the text of a Latin hymn, he related these to the pitches c, d, e, f, g, a.

The evolution of our present-day staff began in the tenth century. A single horizontal line was drawn from the beginning to the end of the chant. This was the first use of a symbol to indicate the pitch of a horizontal line. Placed in front of the line at the beginning of the piece, this symbol was called "clef" after the French word meaning "key."

The single line represented the pitch of f. Later a second line came into use, representing c, five tones above f. In the eleventh century two more lines began to be used. This enabled more pitch levels to be specified. Both the lines and the spaces between them were used to indicate pitch. Then, as today, these four parallel lines were called the staff.

With the development of the four-line staff, pitch could be shown by the position of the note on the staff, rather than by the shape of the note. During the centuries of experimentation with notation, the monks were challenged by the problem of indicating the length of a note. When the development of the staff freed them from the need to indicate pitch by the shape of a note, the monks developed a system of rhythmic notation based on the shapes of notes.

Hollow notes similar to present-day half and whole notes were utilized, as were notes with and without stems. Rest signs to be written on the staff like notes were also developed. These symbols showed the musicians when to be silent and for what length of time.

Eventually measures and bar lines were added to the staff. Dividing the music into measures through the use of bar lines helped the musician to recognize rhythmic patterns and made it easier to read the music. By the fourteenth century, musicians of the church had worked out a system of neumes which could be used to notate sacred music for worship services and the secular music of the minnesingers of the Middle Ages. By the seventeenth century, music notation had developed much as it is today. However, music notation is continually developing. Contemporary composers continue to experiment with more precise ways of notating their musical ideas.

FOURTEENTH-CENTURY NEUMES:

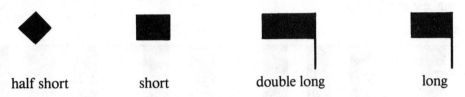

half short   short   double long   long

Understanding Music Notation

Performing music without an understanding of how it is notated is like talking and listening to others without being able to read and write. A literate person communicates in his language through both the spoken and the written word. A knowledge of spelling, grammar, punctuation, and vocabulary enables him to read and write in his language and to speak with others. A knowledge of the symbolic language of music leads to increased musical understanding. It provides the performer with the tools for effective musical communication. An important benefit of musical literacy is the speed and efficiency with which new pieces can be learned.

THE STAFF
The great or grand staff in use today consists of ten horizontal lines. At one time it had eleven lines. It is difficult to read music written on these lines, so the line separating the bass-clef staff and the treble-clef staff is not printed. When the note which belongs on that middle line is used, a short line called a leger line is drawn through the note. This note is called middle C.

A note represents a tone having a certain pitch according to the line or space on which it is placed. Clefs identify the names of the lines and spaces. The bass clef, used for lower voices, is also called the F clef. The head of the F-clef sign rests on the line called F and two dots surround the F line. The treble clef, used for higher voices, is also called the G clef. The end or tail of the symbol circles around the line G. Only the first seven letters of the alphabet are used for pitch names. The pitch names ascend in alphabetical order. The names of the lines and spaces of the bass- and treble-cleff staffs are not the same because of the middle-C line and the space above and below it. Each of these is named in the alphabetical sequence. The bass clef is a lower extension of the treble clef and the treble clef is a higher extension of the bass clef.

Tones within an octave repeat themselves in the next octave. They have the same letter names and are the same pitches, but sound in a higher or lower register.

THE PIANO KEYBOARD
An understanding of how the piano keyboard is organized is helpful in pitch identification. The wide range of notes on the piano makes it the only instrument which encompasses the full range of notated musical pitches. Middle C is a common tone for most voices. It is near the center of the keyboard, to the left of the two black notes below the manufacturer's trademark.

Note the grouping of the black keys into two's and three's. Each black key sounds the pitch a half step above or below the neighboring white key. The black keys take their names from these adjoining white keys. Each black key has two names. The black key to the right of, or above, a neighboring white key shares the same letter name, with a sharp (♯) added. The black key to the left of, or below, a neighboring white key shares the letter name of that key with a flat (♭) added. The distance from any note, black or white, to its nearest neighbor on the keyboard is a half step. Two half steps make a whole step.

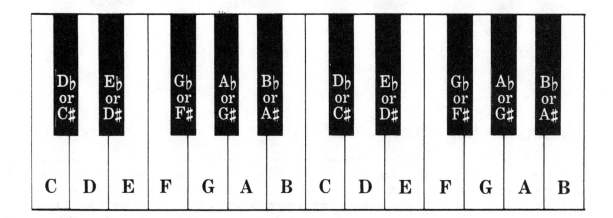

SCALES

Through the centuries of the development of our music system, certain orders of tones sounded pleasing and came to be used over and over. Their function was to provide a tonal structure for the music. At first called modes, they are now usually referred to as scales. This series of tones arranged in a particular ascending or descending order of pitches resembles a musical ladder. In fact, the word "scale" comes from "scala," a Latin word which means "ladder."

The two most frequently used scales in vocal music are the major scale and the minor scale. Each is a series of seven tones within an octave with a special arrangement of half and whole steps. The formula for the order of half and whole steps is consistent for each type of scale, regardless of the starting pitch of the scale.

The scale pattern of half and whole steps for the major scale is:

W W H W W W H

The relative minor is the second tone (letter name) *below* the starting tone for the corresponding major scale. The pattern of half and whole steps for the natural minor is:

W H W W H W W

The C-major scale may be located on the keyboard by looking at the white keys from C to C. Its relative minor is A to A. The formula for each scale is consistent with that listed above.

Scales take their names from their starting note, called the tonic or key tone. The eighth note above or below has the same letter name as the key tone.

Both major and minor scales can be constructed on tones other than C and A; these two scales are the *only* ones which use white notes exclusively. To obtain the proper pattern of half and whole steps for a major or minor scale starting on any other note, the black notes on the keyboard must be used. This means that some of the notes will have flats or sharps by their letter name to indicate the use of a black note.

KEY SIGNATURES

To preserve the correct sequence of intervals for all major scales other than the C-major scale, either flats or sharps must be used. To avoid cluttering up the music with the addition of the necessary flats or sharps by the notes every time they appear in the score, a notational shorthand has been developed. The sharps or flats which will be used are placed to the right of the clef symbol. These flats or sharps alter every note which has the letter name of the line or space on which the flat or sharp is placed, unless a natural sign is used to cancel the flat or sharp.

The sharps or flats which indicate the key signature are always placed in the same order on the staff. Musicians quickly become familiar with the key signatures they use most frequently. Follow these procedures to identify major keys:

FLAT KEYS

The flat (♭) farthest to the right is the 4th note (fa) of the scale. Count down to 1 (do) to find the key.

SHARP KEYS

The sharp (♯) farthest to the right is the 7th note (ti) of the scale. Count up one line or space to 1 to find the key. The name of the key is the letter name of the line or space of 1 or do. If there is a flat (♭) or sharp (♯) in the key signature on that line or space, add that to the name of the key.

RHYTHMIC NOTATION

Meter signatures (time signatures) evolved through several systems over the years. When a musical selection is divided into measures by bar lines, the meter signature tells how many and what kinds of notes may be used in each measure. Placed after the clef along with the key signature, the meter signature tells the number of beats per measure and the kind of note which gets one beat.

Modern music notation utilizes various kinds of notes to show the duration or length of a musical sound. There are corresponding symbols, called rests, which indicate lengths of silence. Notes may be hollow or solid and flags or dots may be added to them. It is important to understand that these symbols represent relative rather than definite times of duration. Tempo (rate of speed) has a role in determining the length of notes within a rhythmic pattern.

Notes and their corresponding rests maintain the same relationship to each other, no matter what kind of note is the unit of beat. Here are the three most commonly encountered types of time signatures:

320

$$\frac{2}{2}(\mathbb{C}) = \frac{2}{\rho} \qquad\qquad \frac{4}{4} = \frac{4}{\rho} \qquad\qquad \frac{6}{8} = \frac{6}{\flat}$$

Study this chart for a better understanding of the relationship of note values in these time signatures:

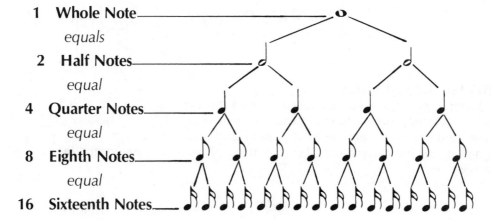

This chart shows relative note and rest values in the notes and rests most often encountered in 4/4 time.

1	Whole Note	𝅝
	equals	
2	Half Notes	𝅗𝅥 𝅗𝅥
	equal	
4	Quarter Notes	♩ ♩ ♩ ♩
	equal	
8	Eighth Notes	♪ ♪ ♪ ♪ ♪ ♪ ♪ ♪
	equal	
16	Sixteenth Notes	𝅘𝅥𝅯 𝅘𝅥𝅯 𝅘𝅥𝅯 𝅘𝅥𝅯 𝅘𝅥𝅯 𝅘𝅥𝅯 𝅘𝅥𝅯 𝅘𝅥𝅯 𝅘𝅥𝅯 𝅘𝅥𝅯 𝅘𝅥𝅯 𝅘𝅥𝅯 𝅘𝅥𝅯 𝅘𝅥𝅯 𝅘𝅥𝅯 𝅘𝅥𝅯

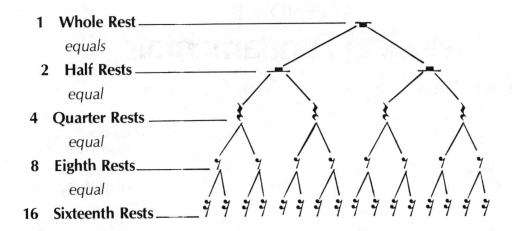

1 **Whole Rest** — *equals*
2 **Half Rests** — *equal*
4 **Quarter Rests** — *equal*
8 **Eighth Rests** — *equal*
16 **Sixteenth Rests** —

EXPRESSIVE MARKINGS

Learning to read music notation provides the performer with information about the pitch and length of tones. The meter and key signature can also be discovered. For an understanding of the tempo and mood of the music, including special instructions on dynamics and articulations, it is necessary for the performer to develop a vocabulary of the words and symbols which give this type of information.

Traditionally, indications for types of moods and various tempos have been given in Italian. Contemporary composers have tended to use more English words, but thanks to our heritage from the Italian musicians of the Renaissance when our notational system was being refined, the vast majority of musical instructions remain in Italian.

These types of markings, terms, and symbols are an important link between composer and performer. It is the responsibility of the performer to learn to speak the musical language used by the composer in order to be true to the composer's intentions.

APPENDIX B
Musical Fundamentals

MUSIC SYMBOLS

322

Staff		D. C.	Da capo (from the beginning)
G (or Treble) clef		D. S.	Dal segno (from the sign)
F (or Bass) clef		𝄋	Sign used for repeat, as in D.S.
Bar line		Fine	The end
Double bar		⊕	Coda mark
Measure			Triplet
Sharp (1/2 step higher)			Duplet
Flat (1/2 step lower)			Tie
Natural (cancels ♯ or ♭)			Slur
Repeat			Fermata (hold)
First and Second endings		ten.	Tenuto (hold) (shorter than ⌢)
		,	Breathing mark (above staff)
		>	Accent
		sfz	Sforzando (sudden strong accent)
			Staccato
			Marcato

NOTES AND RESTS

whole note

whole rest

half-notes

half-rests

quarter-notes

quarter-rests

eighth-notes

eighth-rests

sixteenth-notes

sixteenth-rests

1   2   3   4

Dotted Notes
   The *dot* after a note adds one-half the value of that note to it.

Examples:

Keyboard, Grand Staff, Key Signatures, Scales

Sharp keys with relative minors (natural)

324

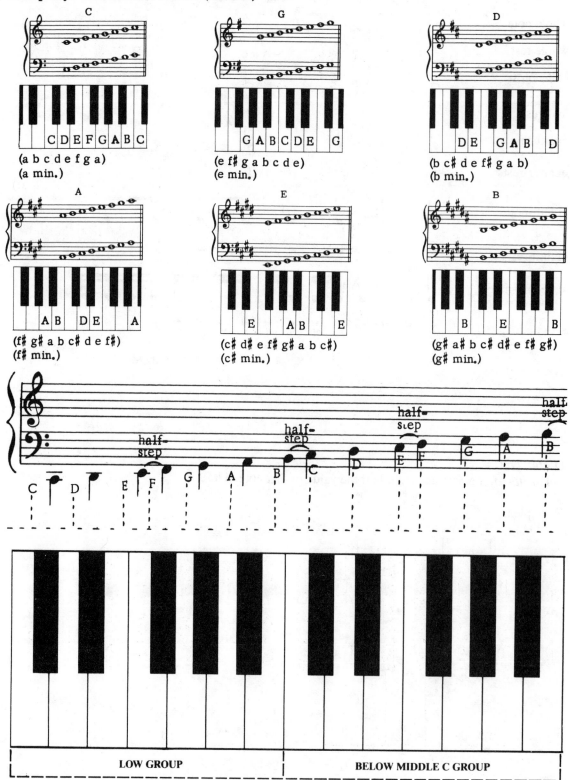

Flat keys with relative minors (natural)

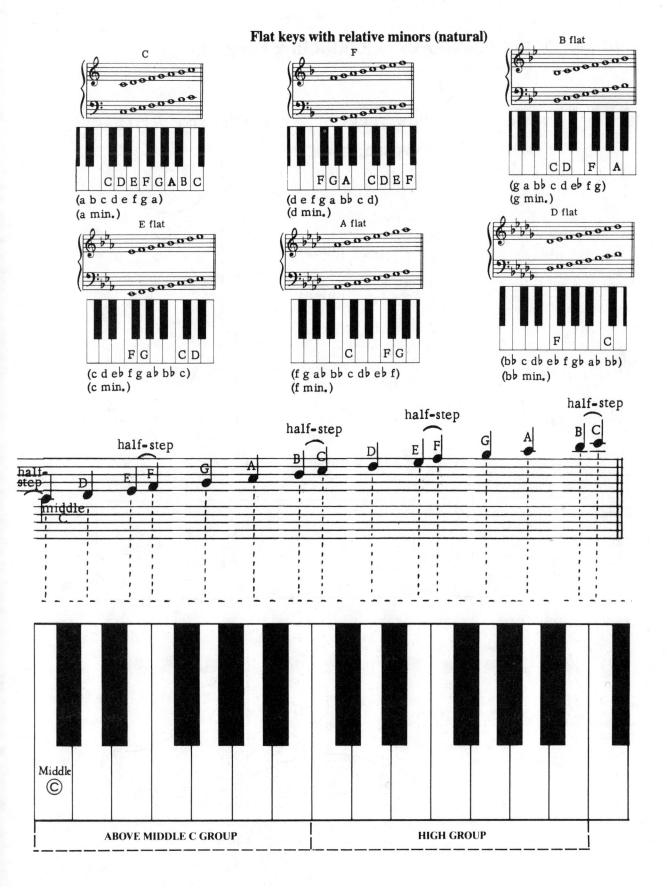

Meter Signatures / Conducting Patterns

METER	COMMON METER SIGNATURES		CONDUCTING PATTERNS
	SIMPLE	COMPOUND	
2	$\frac{2}{2}$ = $\frac{2}{8}$ = $\mathbb{C}$		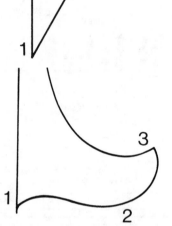
	$\frac{2}{4}$ = $\frac{2}{\rho}$	$\frac{6}{4}$ = $\frac{6}{\rho}$ ($\quad$. = pulse)	
	$\frac{2}{8}$ = $\frac{2}{\beta}$	$\frac{6}{8}$ = $\frac{6}{\beta}$ ($\quad$. = pulse)	
3	$\frac{3}{2}$ = $\frac{3}{8}$		
	$\frac{3}{4}$ = $\frac{3}{\rho}$		
	$\frac{3}{8}$ = $\frac{3}{\beta}$	$\frac{9}{8}$ = $\frac{9}{\beta}$ ($\quad$. = pulse)	

5 and 7	$\frac{5}{4}$ = $\frac{5}{\rho}$ ¦ $\frac{7}{4}$ = $\frac{7}{\rho}$		Conducting Patterns will be in combination depending on pulse grouping
(combination of 2 and 3)	$\frac{5}{8}$ = $\frac{5}{\beta}$ ¦ $\frac{7}{8}$ = $\frac{7}{\beta}$		

4	$\frac{4}{2}$ = $\frac{4}{8}$		
	$\frac{4}{4}$ = $\frac{4}{\rho}$ = C		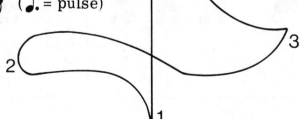
	$\frac{4}{8}$ = $\frac{4}{\beta}$	$\frac{12}{8}$ = $\frac{12}{\beta}$ ($\quad$. = pulse)	

Tempo Markings / Metronomic Markings

very slow	slow	*moderate	fast	very fast
largo lento	andante	*moderato	allegro vivace	
grave adagio	andantino		allegretto	presto

Moderato serves as a good reference tempo since it can be referred to as one's normal walking pace.

Additional terms referring to tempo:

a tempo —return to original tempo
accelerando —go faster; accelerate
allargando —slowing down, usually accompanied by a crescendo
rallentando —gradually slackening in speed
ritardando —gradually slackening in speed
rubato —a certain flexibility of tempo consisting of slight *ritards* and *accelerandos* alternating according to the requirements of musical expression
con moto —with motion
poco più mosso—a little more motion

Common markings referring to metronomes:
1) **Circa (c. or ca.)**—approximately or about
2) **M.M. (or M)**—Maelzel's metronome (or metronome)
3) **M.M.** ♩ = 60—Maelzel's metronome—60 quarter notes per minute
4) **M** ♩ = 44—Metronome—44 half notes per minute
5) ♩ = 68—68 quarter notes per minute
6) ♩ = c. 120—approximately 120 quarter notes per minute

Circle of Fifths

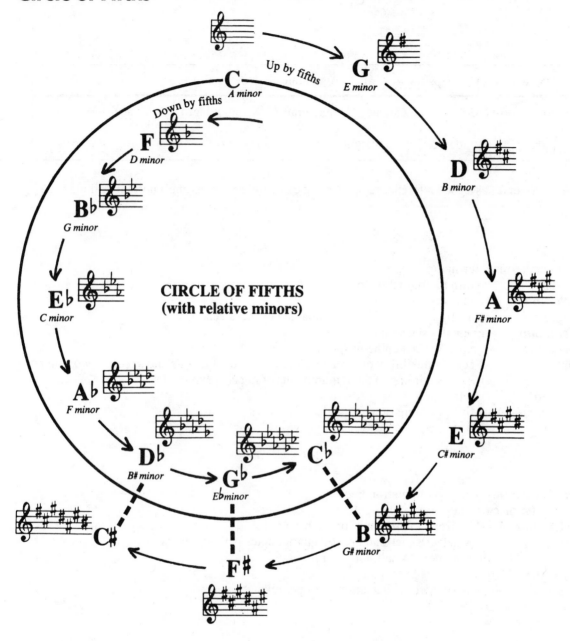

The three pairs of keys at the bottom of the circle are called Enharmonic Keys. They have the same sound, but are spelled differently.

Chords and Cadences

Degrees of the Scale	1	2	3	4	5	6	7	8
Triads	*tonic	supertonic	mediant	*subdominant	*dominant	submediant	leading tone	*tonic
Major Keys	*I	ii	iii	*IV	*V	vi	vii°	*I
Minor Keys (Natural)	*i	ii°	III	*iv	*V	VI	vii°	*i

*Primary Triads (occur most frequently)

with raised 7th of scale

with raised 7th of scale

329

EXAMPLES OF PRIMARY TRIADS

Key of C major

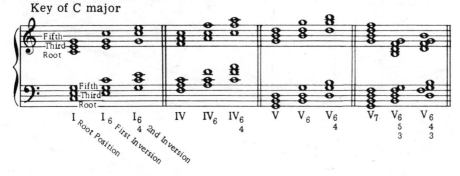

Key of A minor (harmonic)

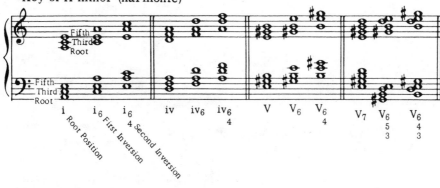

EXAMPLES OF CADENCES   C major

1-2 = Authentic Cadences
3 = Plagal Cadence

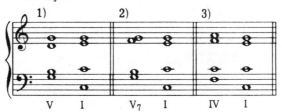

A minor (harmonic)

1-2 = Authentic Cadences
3 = Plagal Cadence

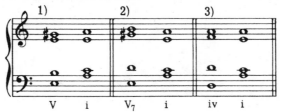

DYNAMICS IN MUSIC

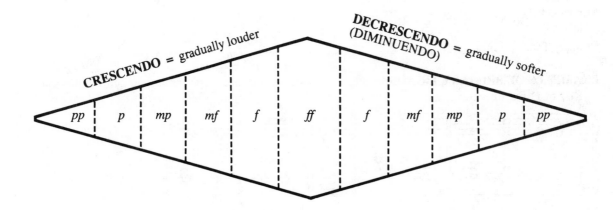

pp—**pianissimo** = very soft

p—**piano** = soft

mp—**mezzo piano** = medium soft

mf—**mezzo forte** = medium loud

f—**forte** = loud

ff—**fortissimo** = very loud

APPENDIX C

Choral Diction and Pronunciation

THE VALUE OF CORRECT DICTION

Vocal and instrumental music have in common the basic musical elements—pitch, rhythm, harmony, timbre, form, and texture. The unique characteristic of vocal music is the *text*. It is a factor in determining how the music should be performed: fast or slow, loud or soft, legato or marcato. In addition to influencing the manner of performance, the text is the means through which the message of the music is communicated to the listeners. The term used for the manner of conveying the meaning of the text to the listener is *diction*.

The concept of diction necessary for singing the music in this text book is not the same as that used by many popular singers. This difference is a matter of style. Each type of music has its own correct style. Performance of the music in this book requires correct vocal diction based on pure vowel sounds and crisp, energetic consonants. The quality of the tone depends a great deal on the thought that is behind the way the tone is produced.

THE VOWEL SOUNDS

When we sing, the sounds that are held or sustained are the vowel sounds. The sustaining of vowel sounds is the primary difference between singing and speaking. Correctly formed vowels can be called "pure vowels." There is a kind of shorthand that can be used to spell these "pure vowel" sounds. These are the symbols from the International Phonetic Alphabet:

ay [e]   ee [i]   ah [a]   oh [o]   oo [u]

Sometimes there are vowels in combinations in words and syllables. When there are two successive vowels in a syllable, it is a diphthong (pronounced "dif-thong"). When there are three successive vowels in a word or syllable, it is a triphthong (pronounced "trif-thong"). Some examples of diphthongs and triphthongs are:

Diphthong		Key Word
[ɑɪ]	as in	*night*
[ɛɪ]	as in	*day*
[ɔɪ]	as in	*boy*
[ɑʊ]	as in	*now*
[oʊ]	as in	*no*
Triphthong		
[ɑɪə]	as in	*ire*
[ɑʊə]	as in	*our*

THE CONSONANT SOUNDS

The combination of vowel sounds with consonants forms words. The element of diction that causes the listener to understand the meaning of the words is the articulation of the consonants. Clearly articulated, rhythmically accurate consonant sounds are essential to correct diction. The singer must allow enough vocal energy to make these sounds. It is important to sing initial consonants which have pitch on the correct pitch, rather than starting under the pitch and sliding to the correct one. The habit of singing these consonants which begin a word under the pitch and the sliding up to the right pitch creates a muddy attack and can result in the entire word being sung under pitch.

FACTORS IN CORRECT DICTION:

1. Clarity. The appropriate pronunciation of the words results from singing correct vowels and consonants. At the same time the words must be clearly enunciated. Mumbled, unprojected words cause the listeners to misunderstand the text and even to lose interest in the choir's performance, regardless of the beauty of the tone. Examples of distorted meanings follow:

Mispronounced Phrase	Correct Meaning
This is a gray country	This is a great country
He is me and my	He is meek and mild

2. Ease. A free, unforced vocal mechanism, characterized by the relaxation of the lips and throat muscles, helps to prevent the distortion of vowel and consonant sounds. The proper use of the lips, teeth, tongue, and jaw promotes the production of desirable vowel and consonant sounds. Here are examples of mispronounced vowels which distort the meaning of the text:

Mispronounced Vowels	Correct Meaning
fur	for
wander	wonder

3. Uniformity. Consistency is a key factor in making a text understandable. If a few singers or even one person changes the pronunciation, the meaning of the text may be unclear. A standard neutral pronunciation, free of regional accent, may be achieved by using the International Phonetic Alphabet as a guide.

4. Accuracy. Precise articulation of consonants will aid rhythmic accuracy and precision. In addition, clarity of the text will be achieved. Some problems in intonation can be corrected through careful attention to consonants.

5. Expressiveness. An important element of expressiveness is the proper use of stressed and unstressed syllables. The monotonous effect of equal stress on all syllables is detrimental to a performance and causes the effect of the text to be lost.

Incorrect Stress	Correct Stress
Je-su joy of man's de-sir-ing	Je-su joy of man's de-sir-ing
The heav-ens are tell-ing	The heav-ens are tell-ing

Music has the unique power to express emotion. Since choral music involves the union of music and text, correct diction can affect the emotional impact of the choir's performance in a positive way. If the text is sung in an unfeeling, careless manner, the choir may expect to receive little more than a polite response from the audience. However, if the text is conveyed to every listener without distortion to reduce the impact of the music, the result will be a source of real satisfaction to both the choir and audience.

APPENDIX D

Sight Reading

For the singer, reading music involves much more than naming notes. In reading words the reader immediately relates to the object or the action implied. Such phrases as "sit in the chair" and "you are my friend," when read either silently or aloud, have instant meaning for the reader. The singer may instantly recognize these notes

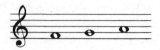

as F G A. However, speaking them — F G A — has no musical meaning. To be read musically the notes must be sounded on the correct pitch (the highness or lowness of a tone). For the pianist or other instrumentalist there is no problem: playing the piano keys or pressing the valves to make the desired pitch can be learned rather quickly. The singer, however, has no keys or valves in his or her throat. He or she must look at the notes on the staff, form a mental concept of their sound, or pitch, then produce those pitches vocally. Singers have another problem: unlike instrumentalists, they must also read the words of the text in the correct rhythm, putting words, pitches, and rhythms together so as to convey the composer's meaning to the listeners.

THE IMPORTANCE OF MUSIC READING

Young singers have a large repertoire of songs learned by rote: the pitches have been played repeatedly on the piano, tape or cassette recording, or phonograph. This seems an easy, although dull, course of action. Continued rote learning of songs keeps the singer at a level of accomplishment comparable to that of the small child to whom stories are read and reread until he or she can exactly repeat the story, even though the printed page itself has no meaning to the child.

One of the important goals of the choral-music curriculum is to offer opportunities for young singers to move beyond the rote level and to become musically literate. Some of the advantages of developing proficiency in music reading are:

1. The ability to learn songs quickly.
2. The development of musical literacy as the printed score becomes more meaningful.
3. The growth of musical independence as the keyboard is less and less often used for giving pitches.
4. The feeling of pride in success attained as the reading skill increases.

SYSTEMS

Three generally recognized systems of music reading are:

1. Fixed *do* - C is *do*, regardless of the key.
2. Movable *do* - *do* is the first degree of the scale of the major key in which the song is written.
3. Numbers - the first degree of the scale of the key in which the song is written is 1.

A minor key has as its tonal center *la* of the relative major scale. In other words, a song in a major key and another song in the relative minor of that key have the same *do*. They share the same key signature, but have different tonal centers — *do* in the major key, *la* in the relative minor key.

Each of the three systems is equally valid. Consistent use of the selected system is the important factor: no system will help you to read music unless it is used regularly. The use of the same system in elementary, middle, and high schools will make the sight reading easier and reduce the amount of rehearsal time spent in practice exercises and drills.

LEARNING TO READ MUSIC

As stated above, learning songs by rote is easy, but not really interesting. Reading music may seem difficult in the early stages but becomes easier as you practice regularly. Some suggestions for developing your skill are given here:

1. Accept the challenge! Approach the reading willingly and positively.
2. Beginning when the school year starts, use a few (five to twelve) minutes of *every* choir rehearsal for rhythmic and melodic reading activities.
3. Concentrate on the printed or director-prepared music score of melodic and rhythmic exercises.
4. Since pitch is less mysterious than generally thought, work to sharpen your sensitivity by centering your effort toward a specific pitch as you begin each rehearsal. (Middle C for treble voices and G above/below middle C for SAT (C) B choirs are particularly useful for this exercise.) Think, then sing the chosen pitch without instrumental assistance. Check for correctness. At first the pitch sung may be far from the desired one, but, with practice, the choir will be able to sing desired pitches with a remarkable degree of accuracy — "plucked out of the air," in a manner of speaking.
5. Concentrate on the musical score: do the notes stay on the same line or space? do they ascend? descend? move from line to line? space to space? line to space? space to line? Along with knowing the names of the notes, noting the direction of their movement is very helpful.
6. Reading note names must be accompanied by correct rhythmic reading. Along with recognition of the various kinds of notes, rests, and meters you will need to practice rhythmic patterns. Use a patschen (leg slap) or tapping (desk or chair) to keep the steady beat while you speak and/or sing the rhythm of the melodic line.
7. Use the selected reading system CONSISTENTLY. Regular use will make it a part of your vocabulary.
8. Use what you learn in the reading exercises when studying your songs. The same melodic and rhythmic patterns are included, with the text added.

Finally, consider the music reading as a basic part of your choir rehearsal. One or two hours *once weekly* will be less effective than 5-12 minutes *daily*.

The following is an example of a procedure for reading a song in your text, p. 00, *Spring Carol*, by Larry A. Christiansen.

SPRING CAROL / Larry A. Christiansen
System: selected
Introduction: SATB / F major / 3 - pulse in one / strophic: two stanzas, refrain, coda / English text / homophonic $\frac{3}{4}$
Focus: basically conjunct / exceptions: one perfect fourth interval in soprano and four instances of perfect fifth in bass / otherwise second and third intervals in all parts / note first and second endings

Using syllables or numbers, practice from a prepared score ascending and descending F-major scale and selected scale intervals. Use inner hearing to *think* those pitches outside your singing range and enter singing at the comfortable pitch.

334

①

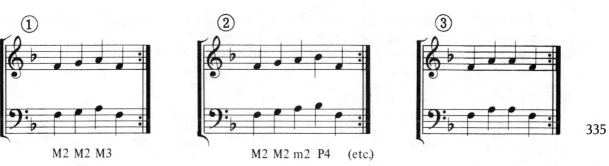
②

③

M2 M2 M3

M2 M2 m2 P4 (etc.)

④

⑤

⑥

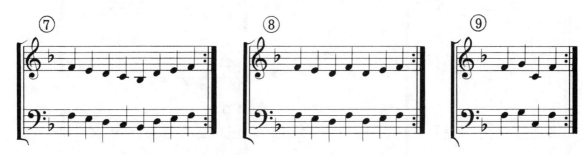
⑦

⑧

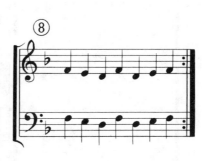
⑨

⑩

⑪

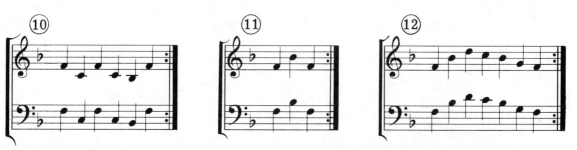
⑫

Study the score of the song, each section on its own part. Discover intervals used in the practice just completed. Sing the intervals again as needed for reinforcement.
Sing these chordal patterns slowly, developing sensitivity to cadential progressions.

Sing these rhythmic patterns on *loo*. Then find those which are included in the song.

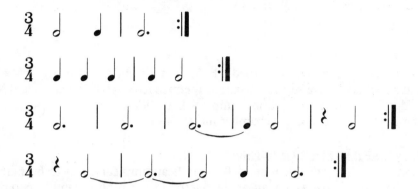

Start a steady, slow patschen or tapping of the steady beat. After it is established (two-four measures) read aloud the words of the entire song in correct rhythm. Use *loo* for the introduction. Maintaining the patschen or tapping of the steady beat, the choir will sing the starting pitches, then the entire song on the chosen syllables or numbers. Avoid stopping! Concentrate! Look ahead! Review any passages which may have caused problems. Note the rit. and a tempo. Then, immediately, sing the entire song with the text. Use a neutral syllable, such as *oo*, for the introduction and the ensuing "humming" measures.

Composer Profiles

ABRAHAM, DIANA (1945-   )

Abraham, who was born in Boston, earned a B.A. in music at the University of Massachusetts and an M.Ed. at New York University. She is currently employed by Bolt, Berenek, and Newman, a leading Cambridge, Mass., communications company. In addition to children's choral music, she is interested in the field of contemporary chamber music.

BACH, JOHANN SEBASTIAN (1685-1750)

Bach inherited a strong family talent and left a significant musical legacy to his many talented children. His long, prolific career began at the age of 15 when he became a choirboy at the Michaeliskirche, Lüneburg, where he began organ lessons. An astoundingly significant career followed at such positions as Weimar (where he wrote the bulk of his organ music), Cöthen (where he composed a great deal of his secular instrumental works), and his final post as cantor at St. Thomas's, Leipzig, where he composed his enormous amount of church music.

Bach's vast musical output contains every kind of music current at the time, except opera. It was written for practical purposes—for the court orchestra, Sunday services, his sons' instruction, his patrons, and his own use.

Bach was a universal musician, whose music has a universal appeal. It is steeped in the flavor of its period, yet belongs to all time.

BRAHMS, JOHANNES (1833-1897)

Johannes Brahms, one of the great composers of the Romantic period, was born in Hamburg, Germany. The son of a double-bass player, at the age of 10, he helped to increase the family's meager income by playing the piano in local taverns. At 14 he made his debut as a pianist but although a gifted performer, his main interest was in composition. His music embraced all forms of composition except opera. In his instrumental music, Brahms deliberately rejected the popular trend of composing "program music" based on legend, folklore, or mythology and set a new trend by writing "absolute music" that was organized according to established musical forms. He became the leader of the movement to restore the Classical traditions of restraint, balance, and objectivity.

Brahms was meticulous and worked slowly and deliberately. He would rewrite or destroy whatever did not measure up to his high standards. This resulted in music of the highest quality. He is an important composer of symphonies, concertos, chamber music, piano music, choral music, and solo songs. *A German Requiem*, written for soprano and baritone solos, chorus, and orchestra, marks his greatest achievement as a choral composer. Other important large works for chorus and orchestra include *Schicksalslied, Gesang der Parzen*, the *Alto Rhapsody, Nänie*, and *Triumphlied*.

In his songs for solo voice or for small ensemble, Brahms is a master, on equal footing with the greatest representatives of the German lied, Franz Schubert (1797-1828) and Robert Schumann (1810-1856). His melodies, inspired by the mood of the poetry, are so perfectly blended to a piano accompaniment that the two are inseparable yet interdependent.

CHRISTIANSEN, LARRY (1941-   )

An attorney, as well as Professor of Music at Southwestern College in Chula Vista, California, Christiansen is a choral composer whose music is published and regularly performed.

DECORMIER, ROBERT (1922-   )

Composer, conductor, and arranger, DeCormier was born in Pinelawn, New York, and educated at Juilliard. He was conductor and arranger to Harry Belafonte and the founder of the Robert DeCormier Singers. He has also arranged a number of Broadway musicals.

DONATO (DONATI), BALDASSARE (ca. 1530-1603)

Donato was born and lived all his life in Venice. His work revolved around St. Mark's Cathedral where he was choirmaster, the most desirable musical post in Italy. His compositions include motets and madrigals.

EHRET, WALTER CHARLES (1918-   )

Born in New York City, Ehret is a composer, author, arranger, and teacher. He was educated at Juilliard. He has had a long career in teaching and is District Coordinator of Music, in the Scarsdale, N.Y., Public Schools. A clinician and lecturer, Mr. Ehret is the arranger of many choral pieces and the author of several textbooks on singing and choral conducting.

GASTOLDI, GIOVANNI GIACOMO (ca. 1556-1622)

An Italian composer, Gastoldi was director of music at the Church of Santa Barbara, the chapel of the Gonzoga family in Mantua, Italy. His work there was exclusively in sacred music. In 1608 he moved to Milan where his work was in secular music only. Gastoldi's fame rests on his many compositions of the balleti, a vocal composition, dancelike in character, which strongly resembles the madrigal. His ballettis were very popular and strongly influenced the great English madrigalist, Thomas Morley. Gastoldi published a five-voice set of ballettis in 1591 which was reprinted ten times in just twenty years.

GRAY, MICHAEL A. (1954-   )

Gray was born in Pasadena and received a B.A. in music at Cal State Fullerton. He is currently a choral teacher and choir director at the Corona-Norco High School. Among his broad activities as a composer and arranger, he is interested in exploring the more advanced techniques of 20th-century choral literature.

HANDEL, GEORGE FRIDERIC (GEORG FRIEDRICH) (1685-1759)

Handel was born in Halle, Germany, the son of a successful barber-surgeon in the court of Saxe-Weissenfels. Although his musical talent surfaced at a very early age, his father did not allow him to practice at the keyboard because he wanted him to become a lawyer. Handel secretly practiced a small clavichord which he smuggled into the attic. Eventually his playing attracted the attention of his father's employer, who convinced his father to allow the boy to study music as well as law. At the age of twelve, Handel became assistant organist of the cathedral in Halle. His musical studies, sponsored by the Duke of Saxe-Weissenfels, included theory, composition, oboe, spinet, harpsichord, and organ.

After a year at Halle University Handel went to Berlin, then to Hamburg as a musician in the opera orchestra. While there he wrote several operas. In 1706 he went to Italy for several years, where he continued to compose. He was associated with the leading patrons and composers of Rome, Florence, Naples, and Venice.

Following a brief return to Germany, he visited England in 1710. He spent the majority of his remaining years in England where he wrote many operas and oratorios as well as some instrumental music. As Director of the Royal Academy of Music, a society organized to promote Italian opera, Handel produced, directed, and wrote operas. As English audiences grew tired of Italian opera, Handel introduced them to oratorio, a sacred work which is performed without scenery, costumes, or action, but which is dramatic in character and usually is based on biblical events. This form had existed before Handel, but it was really just glorified opera. Handel changed the structure of the oratorio by giving greater emphasis to the chorus.

Except for a few brief visits to Germany, Italy, and France, Handel remained in England for forty-seven years. He was very popular with British royalty and was the greatest figure in English music during his lifetime. He was buried with public honors in Westminster Abbey. In spite of the total blindness of his last years he continued to play the organ accompaniment for his oratorios. In fact, he played the *Messiah* a week before his death.

Handel's compositions, both sacred and secular, reveal a spirit of grandeur. Through the immense popularity of his oratorios, he has been recognized as one of the greatest composers of the Baroque age. *Messiah* was his best-known oratorio and is still the most often performed oratorio today.

HAYDN, FRANZ JOSEPH (1732-1809)

An Austrian composer, Haydn was born into a family of twelve children of musical parents. He received musical instruction from the age of five. At eight he was sent to Vienna where he was a chorister at St. Stephen's until his voice changed. After a number of years of struggle to earn a living with his writing, teaching, and performing, he was hired, in 1762, to direct music at the Court of Prince Nikolaus Esterházy. He spent the remainder of his life providing music for the Esterházy Court.

Haydn was acclaimed in Austria as a national hero, and he received many awards, including an honorary Mus.D. degree at Oxford University. His works are among the most popular of all time and included 104 symphonies, chamber music, operas, songs, and oratorios, of which *The Creation* is his most famous.

HAYDN, (JOHANN) MICHAEL (1737-1806)

Five years younger than his brother, Franz Joseph, Michael Haydn was an organist and composer. From the age of eight to eighteen he was a soprano chorister at St. Stephen's, Vienna, following in his brother's footsteps. After service as an organist, violinist, and choir director, he lost his property under the French occupation of Salzburg in 1800. Helped by his brother and friends, including Empress Maria Theresa, who rewarded him for writing a Mass in which she sang the soprano solos, he organized a school of composition and taught some of the leading musicians of the day.

Haydn, a prolific composer, wrote around 400 church compositions (Masses, oratorios, cantatas, requiems, etc.); symphonies, many chamber pieces, divertimentos, dances and marches, and several operas. His greatest works were sacred compositions which were written to satisfy the requirements of the church reformers who wanted to concentrate on choral compositions that were related to church ritual rather than instrumental music and virtuosic solo singing. Haydn also pleased the reformers by editing a simplified hymnal. Because he was overshadowed by his brother's fame and because his works were not published until after his death, his excellent music is only now becoming recognized.

HUMPERDINCK, ENGELBERT (1854-1921)

A German composer, Humperdinck was studying architecture in Cologne when he was persuaded to devote himself to music. After winning prizes for his compositions, he visited Italy where he met Richard Wagner and became a friend of the Wagner family. After several years as a music teacher, he turned completely to composition. His best-known work is the two-act opera *Hansel and Gretel*, which shows his skill in combining Wagnerian harmony with folklike melodies.

KAPLAN, ABRAHAM (1931-   )

Born in Tel Aviv, Kaplan is a composer, conductor, and Ed. professor. He was educated at the Israel Academy, Jerusalem, and the Juilliard School of Music. He was the conductor of the Kol

Israel Chorus and the guest conductor with major symphony orchestras. Founder and conductor of the Camerata Singers in New York, he has been director of choral music at Juilliard and director of orchestra, chorus, and opera at the University of Washington, Seattle. His compositions include vocal and instrumental works.

KIRK, THERON (1919-   )

Born in Alamo, Texas, Kirk studied composition with Bernard Rogers and Karel Jirak and at Baylor University. He has received ASCAP awards, the Benjamin award, and the Phi Mu Alpha Sinfonia Orpheus award in 1976. Since 1965 he has been a professor at San Antonio College. In addition to many choral works, including cantatas, he has written a one-act comic opera and band and orchestal works.

KOUNTZ, RICHARD (1896-1950)

A native of Pittsburgh, Kountz worked in radio broadcasting in that city. He was later associated with the M. Witmark Publishing Company. His compositions include songs, organ pieces, and choral works.

LASSO, ORLANDO DI (c. 1532-1594)

Born in Mons, Belgium, di Lasso was trained as a choirboy in the service of the church. His voice was so beautiful that he was kidnapped three times in vain attempts to secure him as a singer in various churches. Di Lasso's singing career took him first to Sicily in the service of Ferdinando Gonzaga, viceroy of Sicily. When Gonzaga was transferred, di Lasso went with him, first to Palermo and then to Milan. Eventually he was appointed to the court of Albert V of Bavaria in Munich. He is known by several names: Roland de Lassus (Belgian), Orlando di Lasso (Italian), Orlandus Lassus (Latin), and Rolande de Lattre (French). He was knighted by both Emperor Maximilian II and the Pope.

One of the most prolific and versatile of all Renaissance vocal composers, di Lasso was called the "Belgian Orpheus" and the "Prince of Music." His importance as a composer lies in the fact that his music embraces the flavor and style of several countries. He was a master composer of Italian madrigals, German lieder, French chansons, and Latin motets. He wrote over 2,000 works (all vocal), representing every style of vocal music of his time: 53 Masses, 500 motets, 133 French chansons, 100 Magnificats, numerous Italian madrigals, German lieder, and 7 Penitential Psalms.

LAWRENCE, STEPHEN (1939-   )

Lawrence was born in New York City and educated at Hofstra University. He is a composer of songs and film and television scores.

LUTKIN, PETER CHRISTIAN (1858-1931)

Born in Wisconsin, Lutkin studied music in Chicago, Berlin, Paris, and Vienna. He was an organist and one of the founders of the American Guild of Organists. After teaching theory at the American Conservatory of Music (Chicago) and Northwestern University, he was Dean of the Northwestern School of Music from 1897 until his death.

MENOTTI, GIANCARLO (1911-   )

An Italian composer who came to the United States in 1928, Menotti is well known for his Christmas opera *Amahl and the Night Visitors*, written in 1951. His awards include the Lauber composition prize and Pulitzer prizes. He taught at the Curtis Institute in Philadelphia, then became organizer and director of the Spoleto Festivals in Italy and the United States. He continues to be a prolific composer of works which include operas and, orchestral, chamber, and choral compositions. At present he lives in Scotland.

MONTEVERDI (Monteverde), CLAUDIO (1567-1643)

The eldest son of a doctor, Monteverdi studied with Ingegneri. Before being ordained as a priest in 1632, he held numerous musical posts including St. Mark's in Venice.

His church music includes 3 Masses, Vespers, Magnificats, and numerous motets as well as much secular vocal music. The church music may be divided into two contrasted groups, one in the traditional polyphonic style, while the other adopts the new Baroque methods of expressive writing for solo voices and choruses with effective use of instrumental resources.

For the stage he wrote at least 12 operas (only 3 of which survive complete) and ballets.

MORLEY, THOMAS (1557-c. 1602)

A pupil of William Byrd, Morley was organist at St. Paul's Cathedral in 1591 before becoming a gentleman of the Chapel Royal the next year. He was granted a monopoly of music printing but later assigned that to Thomas East in 1600.

Published works include canzonets, madrigals, balletts, consort lessons, and ayres. His *Plaine and Easie Introduction to Practicall Musicke* (1597) was the first comprehensive treatise on composition printed in England.

PAGE, ROBERT E. (1927-   )

Born in Abilene, Texas, Page received his B.A. in music from Abilene Christian (Magna Cum Laude), his M.M. from Indiana University, and an honorary D. Mus. from Beaver College in Philadelphia. He has been Director of Choruses of the Cleveland Orchestra for thirteen years, as well as an assistant conductor of that orchestra, and is Musical Director of the Mendelssohn Choir of Pittsburgh. He is also currently active as a choral arranger and composer.

PALESTRINA, GIOVANNI PIERLUIGI DA (c. 1525-1594)

Giovanni Pierluigi da Palestrina takes his name from his birthplace, Palestrina, a small town near Rome. His entire professional career, from his days as a choirboy at Santa Maria Maggiore to his appointment as "Maestro di cappella" of the Julian Chapel in St. Peter's, was spent in Rome in the service of the Church. He has been called "The Prince of Music" and his works are regarded today, as they were in his own day, as supreme examples of the proper liturgical style. Based largely on elements drawn from the Franco-Flemish style, the core of Palestrina's style is imitative counterpoint. The voice parts flow in continuous rhythm, with a new melodic motive for each new phrase of the text. Palestrina's modal melodies, often built on themes from Gregorian chant, are basically stepwise. They have few repeated notes, move within the limited range of a ninth, are easily singable, and exhibit a natural, elegant curve of sound. Harmony, rhythm, and form are also treated with care and restraint; but it is the text which governs the musical organization of his works. His sensitivity to it is evident in his use of pictorial imagery and absolute dedication to proper word accentuation.

Palestrina's works include 92 Masses, 600 motets, psalms, hymns, and a number of secular madrigals.

PRAETORIUS, MICHAEL (1571-1621)

A foremost German composer and theorist, he was one of the most versatile and prolific musicians of his time. Like Hassler, he practiced the elaborate polychoral style of composition cultivated in Venice. In addition to his extensive list of compositional output he wrote three volumes entitled *Syntagma musicum*, dealing respectively with (1) the origins of liturgical and secular music, (2) a detailed account of instruments and their function, and (3) the notation and methods of performance and principles of choir training in the 17th century.

RICHAFORT, JEAN (ca. 1480-1548)

Not much is known about the life of the Franco-Flemish composer, Jean Richafort. His professional career included appointments as Music Director at St. Rombaud in Mechelen, at St. Gilles in

Bruges, and at the French royal chapel. He was also a singer at the French royal chapel. It is assumed that he was a student of Josquin des Prez. His works, all vocal, include three Masses, over twenty-five motets, chansons, and several secular motets.

RICHTER, CLIFFORD G. (1917-   )

Born in Pittsburgh, Richter was educated at the Dalcroze School of Music. His career has included teaching in colleges and editing for music publishers. As a violist, he has played with orchestras and chamber music groups. He was the organizer and music director of the American Bach Society in Rockland County, New York. His compositions include some choral works; he has also served as translator of many choral texts.

RIEGGER, WALLINGFORD (1885-1961)

Born in Albany, Georgia, Riegger was raised in Indianapolis and New York City. One of two sons of musical parents, Riegger studied violin, piano, and harmony, later changing to cello in order to play in a family string quartet. He was educated at Cornell, the Institute of Musical Art in New York, and the Academy of Music in Berlin. He performed and made his debut as a conductor in Germany, even conducting without music, an uncommon practice in 1910. He played in the St. Paul Symphony and later taught at Drake University in Iowa, the Ithaca Conservatory, Ithaca, New York, and the Metropolitan Music School in New York City, where he was later made president.

He was a prominent member of a group of American avant-garde composers who promoted the performance of contemporary music. In his own compositions, Riegger moved from quasi-impressionism to atonal and twelve-tone music.

Riegger wrote symphonies, chamber music, ballets, and many songs, some published under various names. He received many commissions and awards, among them the Elizabeth Sprague Coolidge Prize, the New York Music Critics Circle Award, and honorary doctorates in music from the Cincinnati Conservatory (1925) and Bard College, Annandale, New York, in 1961.

SACCO, JOHN (1905-   )

Born and educated in New York (B.A. Columbia, and M.A. Columbia Teacher's College) Sacco is a composer, conductor, and pianist. Principally a song and choral composer, his songs were widely performed by Gladys Swarthout and James Melton.

SAINT-SAËNS, CHARLES CAMILLE (1835-1921)

Born in Paris, Saint-Saëns, gave his first piano concert at the age of ten. He became an outstanding pianist and organist. After about twenty years as a church organist in Paris, he toured Europe as a pianist and conductor. He performed in Russia, England, and the United States, and, at the age of eighty-one, appeared in several cities in South America.

Although Saint-Saëns wrote more than 200 compositions, not too many are performed today, among them the opera, *Samson et Dalila*; the tone poem, *Danse macabre*; a work for two pianos and orchestra, *Carnival of the Animals*, and some symphonies and concertos.

SCHILLIO, EMILE JACQUES (1909-   )

A composer, arranger, and orchestrator, Schillio was born in London. He was educated at the National Conservatory of Paris, Loyola University, and California State University. As a performer he has been violinist with Publix-Paramount, the New Orleans Symphony Orchestra, where he was assistant concert master, and the Fort Worth Symphony Orchestra. His compositions include songs and instrumental works.

SCHUMAN, WILLIAM HOWARD (1910-   )

One of America's most eminent composers, Schuman has also had a unique and distinguished career as an educator, administrator, and executive.

Soon after earning a B.A. and M.A. at Columbia Teacher's college, studies at the Mozarteum

Academy in Salzburg, and private studies with Roy Harris, he attracted the attention of Koussevitzky who gave the first performance of his *American Festival Overture* with the Boston Symphony Orchestra in 1939. He was recipient of the first Pulitzer Prize in music for the cantata, *A Free Song*. Subsequently, he taught at Sarah Lawrence College, was Director of Publications at G. Schirmer, Inc., and President of The Juilliard School of Music until 1962. From 1962 to 1969 he was President of Lincoln Center for the Performing Arts in New York. He has also received the Composition Award of the American Academy of Arts and Letters, and two Guggenheim Fellowship Awards.

He has composed an opera (*The Mighty Casey*, revised as a cantata, *Casey At the Bat*), chamber music, concertos, a ballet, music for solo piano, band, chorus, and ten symphonies. He continues to be performed worldwide by the leading orchestras, ensembles, and soloists of our time.

SMITH, GREGG (1931-   )

Founder and Director of the internationally acclaimed Gregg Smith Singers, Smith is also a highly productive composer. Since earning his Master's Degree in composition from U.C.L.A. in 1956 with a choral cantata, he has composed copiously in many media. Within the past few years he has produced a ballet for orchestra, a large magnificat for chorus, a lullaby for soprano and orchestra, some 20 smaller choral works, and three large orchestral works.

The Singers, who possess one of the broadest repertories of any choral group in the world, are particularly reknowned for their pioneering work in the music of Schoenberg and Ives, as well as a close personal association with Stravinsky.

STICKLES, WILLIAM (1882-1971)

Born in Cohoes, New York, Stickles was educated at the Utica, N.Y., Conservatory and Syracuse University. He taught voice in Florence, Italy, Boston, and New York City. He was the composer of a number of songs.

TREHARNE, BRYCESON (1879-1948)

A composer, producer, and educator, Treharne was born in Wales and died in New York City. After his education at the Royal College of Music, London, he taught at the University of Adelaide, Australia. He then lived in Canada and the United States. He spent two years in a German prison camp in World War I. A recipient of an honorary Music Doctorate from McGill University, his compositions include songs and instrumental works.

TRUSLER, IVAN (1879-1948)

Born in Arkansas, Trusler was educated at the Kansas State Teachers College and Columbia University. After a number of years in public school and church music, he was Director of Choral Organizations at the University of Delaware. He is a choral arranger.

VICTORIA, TOMÁS LUIS de (1549-1611)

Sixteenth-century Spain evokes memories of Philip II, possibly the most ardent religious figure ever to reign over a great empire. It is then fitting that the chief composer of his reign, Tomás Luis de Victoria, should also display such singleness of purpose in his own life. Born in Avila, Victoria was an ordained priest; he only wrote music for the Church; he studied in Rome, the capital of the Christian world; and his entire life was spent in service to the Church.

In technical mastery of vocal polyphony and in his devotion to a religious ideal, Victoria's music closely resembles that of his older contemporary, Palestrina. But Palestrina's music embodies a conservative, inward, pure and almost abstract expression, while Victoria's music is generally more zealous and boldly imaginative.

WILDER, ALEC (1907-1980)

A composer and arranger, Wilder was born in Rochester, New York and studied at the Eastman School of Music. He received numerous awards: from ASCAP; the Deems Taylor award; National Endowment for the Arts grants; a Guggenheim fellowship. Along with works for the theater, he wrote instrumental music for many solo performers and chamber groups.